Home Therapy

Home Therapy

FAST, EASY, AFFORDABLE MAKEOVERS

LAURI WARD

G. P. PUTNAM'S SONS
NEW YORK

G. P. PUTNAM'S SONS
Publishers Since 1838
Published by the Penguin Group

Penguin Group (USA) Inc., 375 Hudson Street, New York, New York 10014, USA
Penguin Group (Canada), 90 Eglinton Avenue East, Suite 700, Toronto, Ontario M4P 2Y3, Canada (a division of Pearson Penguin Canada Inc.)
Penguin Books Ltd, 80 Strand, London WC2R 0RL, England
Penguin Ireland, 25 St Stephen's Green, Dublin 2, Ireland (a division of Penguin Books Ltd)
Penguin Group (Australia), 250 Camberwell Road, Camberwell, Victoria 3124, Australia (a division of Pearson Australia Group Pty Ltd)
Penguin Books India Pvt Ltd, 11 Community Centre, Panchsheel Park, New Delhi–110 017, India
Penguin Group (NZ), Cnr Airborne and Rosedale Roads, Albany, Auckland 1310, New Zealand (a division of Pearson New Zealand Ltd.)
Penguin Books (South Africa) (Pty) Ltd, 24 Sturdee Avenue, Rosebank, Johannesburg 2196, South Africa

Penguin Books Ltd, Registered Offices: 80 Strand, London WC2R 0RL, England

ILLUSTRATIONS BY WILLIAM D. CROSSAN
Photographs on pages 26–27; 30–31; 68; 69; 86–87; 88; 152; 153; 184–85; 190–91; 208–9; 212; 213; 232; 251; 253; 254–55; 257; 267; 268–69 by Frances Janisch
Photograph on pages 278–79 © 2004 Joseph Lapeyra
Photograph on page 81 by Tara Duff-Cloes
Photographs on page 82 by John Duff and Brian Levy
Additional photographs by Lauri Ward
Photograph on page 11 by Tim Macht
Photograph on page 23 by Jay Nubile
Photograph on page 63 by Arthur Tasker
Photograph on page 145 by Fred Miller
Photograph on page 159 courtesy Susan Ollila

Library of Congress Cataloging-in-Publication Data

Ward, Lauri.
    Home therapy : Fast, easy, affordable makeovers / Lauri Ward.
      p.   cm.
    ISBN 0-399-15296-2
    1. Interior decoration—Handbooks, manuals, etc.   I. Title.
NK2115.W194   2005   2005042951
747'.88—dc22

Printed in the United States of America
10 9 8 7 6 5 4 3 2 1

This book is printed on acid-free paper. ∞

Book design by DEBORAH KERNER • DANCING BEARS

While the author has made every effort to provide accurate telephone numbers and Internet addresses at the time of publication, neither the publisher nor the author assumes any responsibility for errors or for changes that occur after publication. Further, the publisher does not have any control over and does not assume any responsibility for author or third-party websites or their content.

In loving memory of my father,

David F. Rovin,

and my little brother,

Robert J. "Bobby" Rovin,

and the songs

we sang together
in sweet harmony.

Acknowledgments

To all of the Use What You Have® clients who have so generously shared their stories and homes with me and who made this book possible, thank you very much. I am most grateful to you for allowing my readers to come in and visit.

Many thanks to the readers of *Use What You Have® Decorating* and *Trade Secrets from Use What You Have® Decorating*, with special thanks to those of you who have taken the time to send letters and e-mail sharing anecdotes about how your transformed homes have changed your lives. You have changed mine.

Eternal thanks to my husband, Joe Ward, for making my dreams come true. My best friend and hero, he continues to make our life together great fun, and I am indebted to him for all that he does for Use What You Have®, Inc., and the Interior Refiners Network®, especially in the areas of production and technology. He is truly the driving force behind our business.

Thanks to my wonderful daughter, Tracy Taylor Ward, who is so supportive, loving, and my greatest joy. Now that she has reached adulthood, I hope we will work together, as she has always been my go-to person for a firm second opinion on decorating matters. Whichever career path she chooses—interior refinement, music, or television—I believe in her and her ability.

Thank you, thank you to Liv and Bill Blumer of the Blumer Literary Agency. Liv, a world-class agent, provides incredible feedback and support, and her terrific ideas are always right on the money. Bill does a great job of dealing with the contracts and handling the many details that keep things running smoothly. For all this, and for our friendship, I am grateful.

Thank you very much to my editor, John Duff, for the vision he has had for my books and for making our projects together so pleasurable. Perhaps it is because John is able to do for books what I try to do for rooms that we have such a synergetic relationship. I am truly appreciative of all his support over the years.

Many thanks to Judy Kern for her help with getting my manuscript into good shape. Always a pro, she patiently hung in there as I kept honing and switching around chapters. Based upon her editorial suggestions, she, at times, seems able to read my mind.

Thanks again to Bill Crossan for his skillful, detailed illustrations and for understanding how important it is to accurately show readers every element in each room.

Thank you to everyone at Putnam for their fine work, especially Marilyn Ducksworth, director of corporate public relations, Lisa Amoroso for the smart jacket design, Deborah Kerner for the wonderful book design, and Adrienne Schultz, assistant editor, for all of her help.

Thanks very much to sweet Frances Janisch for her beautiful photographs. It is always a pleasure to work with her. And thanks to Joe Lapeyra too.

My deep gratitude goes to the team at Use What You Have®, Inc., for making our clients happy. As a result of your efforts we are able to transform hundreds of homes every year.

My heartfelt thanks go to all of the talented, certified members of the Interior Refiners Network®, the preeminent organization of one-day redecorators and redesigners throughout the United States and in Canada, Mexico, Europe, and Australia. Their passion and commitment to providing affordable decorating help by involving, informing, and inspiring the public, using the original Use What You Have® system, is awesome and I am honored to have trained them.

Very special thanks to Maria (Amanda) Santisteban Sanchez, Troy Morrison, and Catriona Stuart. I truly appreciate all of their help over the years.

A final thank you to some of my favorite stores where I can always find special things: Gracious Home, The Finished Room, Bedford & Company, and KA International, all in New York City, and Tuvalu in Laguna Beach, California.

Contents

Introduction   1

The Ten Most Common Decorating Mistakes   7

1. **A Call for Style**: Making a Home Feel Like One's Own   11

2. **Downsizing Downtown**: Moving to a Smaller Space   23

3. **Home Alone!** Life After Roommates   33

4. **Furniture the Size of Texas**: Accommodating a Transfer   43

5. **Clearing the Clutter**: Coming to Terms with an Overstuffed Home   51

6. **Serviceable and Stylish**: Creating a Home Office   63

7. **Lost in Translation**: Switching from Renting to Owning   71

8. **Room to Grow**: More Space, More Challenges   81

9. **Better Safe than Sorry**: Childproofing with Style   91

10. **Life Goes On**: New Career, New Pets, New Look   99

11. **Country Goes City**: Moving from a House to an Apartment   111

12. **Living Well in Limbo**: Making the Best of a Temporary Rental   119

13. **Staying On While Moving Up**: Putting an End to the Dormitory Look   135

14. **Playful Elegance:** Seeking Formality in a Child-Friendly Space 145

15. **An Eye for Detail:** Completing an Art Collector's Home 159

16. **Making Bigger Better:** Redesigning an Unused Extension 177

17. **Decorating Détente:** Putting All the Pieces Together, at Long Last 195

18. **Preparing for Baby and Buyers:** Getting Resale-Ready™ 215

19. **Easy Listening:** Living with a Very Grand Piano 227

20. **Artist in Residence:** Longtime Art Collectors Take Stock 235

21. **Views on Retirement:** Moving from Coast to Coast 245

22. **Design for Love:** Merging Households 259

23. **Solid Roots:** Making a Commitment to Stay and Redecorate 271

24. **Breathing Room:** Creating a Home Sanctuary 281

25. **Bedtime Story:** Seeking a Serene Environment 295

Home Therapy

Introduction

Our homes reflect who we are. When we invite someone into our living space, we're revealing ourselves, and if we're not happy with what we show, or if we feel it isn't a true reflection of who we are, we're uncomfortable. We're reminded of that discomfort each time we walk through our own front door. And, to make matters worse, we may even avoid inviting other people into our homes and, therefore, into our lives.

I can't recount how many people have told me that they've always been self-conscious about inviting anyone over because they were worried about what their family and friends would think. It's not that they were trying to impress; it's just that their home didn't reflect who they really are.

In this book, you'll be meeting many of those people, from a couple who feared that their inability to merge their belongings compatibly somehow reflected incompatibility on a deeper level to a man who was reclaiming his living space from a series of roommates, a couple with a new baby and plans to find a new home to an avid collector looking for ways to enjoy her stuff without feeling overwhelmed by it.

People call Use What You Have® for a variety of reasons, depending on their circumstances and what's happening in their lives at the moment. Sometimes they put off making the call, as was the case of the ninety-three-year-old gentleman who told me he'd

1

intended to contact us about ten years before but hadn't bothered because he was sure he would die soon. But, he told me, he was still alive and still muttering under his breath about the way his home looked, so he finally picked up the phone. "You'd better come soon," he said when we spoke. "The way things are going I may live to be one hundred, and this place is still annoying me."

And then there was the woman who called shortly after losing both of her parents in quick succession. She told me that they'd always complained that her place was "a wreck," and now she wanted to redecorate both as a distraction from her grief and as "insurance," just in case, as she said, "they're looking down on me."

Before people make that call, however, they must perceive that they have a problem. In other words, like people who make an appointment with their doctor, they know something just isn't right. And, as with  a physical problem, the diagnosis may be more or less obvious, even to them, but they are looking for a confirmation. Perhaps they're moving from a larger to a smaller space, like the couple who had relocated to New York City with a houseful of "Texas-size" furniture or the gentleman moving from a traditional one-bedroom home to a much smaller studio. Or they may simply feel that their rooms are not as pulled-together as they could be and don't know how to get the look they want. In fact, they may not even know exactly what that "look" should be. In that case, the first thing they're likely to say when I walk in the door is "Lauri, help me! I just don't know what to do with this place."

▶ Our homes are filled with things handed down by beloved family members, things we've acquired at various stages in our lives, even things that symbolize a certain degree of financial success. In other words, we live not only with our furnishings and accessories but with a lot of baggage as well. And, unlike clothing, which we tend to wear out or discard with some regularity, we can get bogged down by our attachment to these more permanent possessions. As a result, even though we'd like to think of our living space as making an accurate statement about who we are, very often, at some point, we come to realize that it's really a reflection of someone we once were but might not be any longer.

As a design consultant, I've had the privilege of working with thousands of people at every stage of life, and because I specialize in using what people have, I get a pretty good idea of who they are and what they like within moments of walking through the door. People's "stuff" and the stories they tell me about that stuff—why they have it, where they got it, and what they do or don't like about it—let me know a great deal about them in a very short time. That, in turn, lets me know what they need and how I can help them to get it.

They may be starting with an empty space, like the couple who purchased their dream retirement home on the California coast. They may be willing to replace almost everything, like the woman who told me she was ready to ditch everything in the living room except her piano. Or they may want to keep as much as possible, making only minimal new purchases. No matter what their situation, however, they are looking to me to help them determine how to use whatever they have, literally and figuratively, in the best possible way.

Unlike more traditional designers, my mission, that of Use What You Have® and that of the Interior Refiners Network, the international organization of designers I'm proud to have founded, is to help each one of these people achieve their personal vision—whatever that may be. We believe it is

3

our mandate to involve, inform, and inspire our clients in order to help them reach their full potential. And sometimes that means we have to begin by helping them to figure out or define what they want because they're not really quite sure. The "refinement" of their rooms is our way of helping them to create a living space that clearly and accurately reflects their individual and unique taste, interests, personality, and lifestyle. Instead of asking our clients to leave their home so that we can "surprise" them with the results *we think they want*, we work side by side with them so that we can educate them about decorating and, at the same time, get their reactions to our suggestions. By doing that, we learn what they do and don't like, which helps to ensure their satisfaction. As a result of this kind of collaboration, our consultations, more often than not, go way beyond the discussion of lighting, painting, and sofa styles.

In the end, what we all strive for is to help people get what they need from their environment so they'll feel that their home is an accurate outward reflection of who they are on the inside. In that way, we actually can help them improve their lives—often in the space of one day and at very little cost.

In the following pages, you'll meet people from all walks of life who have called me in for reasons as diverse as the birth of a baby, the need for tranquillity after a life-altering traumatic experience, the desire to achieve a more sophisticated look that reflects their personal development, and the frustration of having spent many thousands of dollars on a renovation that failed to achieve its intended purpose.

You'll learn not only what triggered their call for help but also something about them as people, so that you'll be able to see how their personal issues intersect with their perceived decorating problems. You'll hear their initial complaints, their ultimate reactions, and which of my suggestions surprised them the most, those "I never would have thought of that" ideas that inevitably come up in the course of every consultation.

In some instances we needed only one "therapy" session to rectify the problem; in others we were able to create significant immediate changes with a few longer-term adjustments required, and in some cases—if, for example, the client was moving into an empty space or would actually be replacing a significant portion of what she or he had—we did nothing at all that first day except to create the design plan that would lead to the ultimate transformation. In every one of the twenty-five scenarios, you'll see before-and-after photographs of the rooms we redid, and in ten of them, we'll return to the scene for an updated view of what the client accomplished after our first meeting.

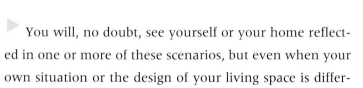

You will, no doubt, see yourself or your home reflected in one or more of these scenarios, but even when your own situation or the design of your living space is different from any one of the places featured here, I believe you'll be able to glean lots of hints, tips, and practical ideas that will help you to make your own home—whatever its style, size, or location—reflect a clearer, more accurate, and, above all, more comfortable and satisfying view of who you are today, whatever your stage of life, your circumstances, and your personal needs.

THE TEN MOST COMMON DECORATING MISTAKES

In all my years of experience, I've found that if clients are unhappy with their living space, it's because they've made one or more of ten common decorating mistakes.

If you are familiar with my work or with my previous books, you will no doubt already know these most common mistakes and should feel free to skip right to the next section. If you are new to Use What You Have®, I present them here because you'll be seeing them time and again in the pages that follow.

Not every one of the clients whose homes are featured in *Home Therapy* has actually made these mistakes because some of them are moving into empty spaces. In those instances, however, they've called me in to ensure that they'll "get it right the first time" without costly investments that might then have to be fixed or undone.

As you read, you'll become more familiar with the principles that underlie the reasons for my calling them "mistakes," and you'll become more adept at spotting them when you look at the "before" photos in these makeovers.

1. Not defining your priorities

Before you begin, you need to determine your needs and your budget, which might be based on whether you rent or own your home, who lives there, and how long you intend to stay.

2. An uncomfortable conversation area

Are people able to sit facing one another? Can they chat without raising their voices? The ideal conversation area is U-shaped; the least desirable, because it is the most uncomfortable, is L-shaped. And beware of the dreaded sofa/loveseat combination!

3. Poor furniture placement

Avoid pressing all your furniture up against the walls as if there were a dance floor cleared in the middle, but also make sure you can pass through the room unobstructed by pieces of furniture.

4. A room that is off-balance

A room is off-balance when all the large, heavy pieces are on one side and the smaller, more delicate pieces on another.

5. Furniture of different heights

When seating is of different heights, and/or artwork is hung on different levels, the effect creates a "roller coaster" that causes the eye to travel uncomfortably up and down around the room.

6. A room that lacks cohesion

The quickest and easiest way to achieve a cohesive "pulled-together" look is to use pairs—of chairs, lamps, end tables, and so on—and, no, it's not boring!

7. Ignoring the focal point of the room

A focal point can be a fireplace, a window with an interesting or attractive view, a large painting or group of pictures, or even a television in the family room—in effect, whatever is most eye-catching in the space. Once you've determined the focal point, it's important to "play it up" so that it attracts the eye, rather than minimize it so that attention is drawn elsewhere (or nowhere in particular).

8. Improper use of artwork

Hanging art too high and/or scattering it on every wall are two of the ways people most often display their artwork incorrectly. Art is best hung about three inches lower than you'd normally think is correct—generally below what you consider "eye level"—and one wall should always be left bare to give the eye a place to rest.

9. Ineffective use of accessories

Over time, most people have accumulated more knickknacks than they have room to display, and some of them should probably be kept out of sight in any case. When it comes to accessories, one should gather like items together as collections and display only the best and most attractive of what one has. These displays can be rotated seasonally or even annually, if necessary, to give each accessory its due, so to speak, but as a general rule, less is more.

10. Using lighting incorrectly

Each room needs task lighting, general illumination, and, in some cases, accent lighting for artwork. Many people make the mistake of underutilizing the lamps they have by using 60-watt bulbs instead of three-way bulbs that go up to 150 watts. General lighting should be directed down where needed rather than up to the ceiling so that it illuminates the entire room without casting shadows or creating too much glare.

A Call for Style

MAKING A HOME FEEL LIKE ONE'S OWN

Laurie Abraham with her daughter, Edie

The Client and the Complaint

"My New York friends' homes seem so stylish," Laurie Abraham admitted somewhat sheepishly the first time we met. "I just want this place to look less bland and to reflect more of the sophistication that I think I've achieved in other aspects of my life."

The way I met this client was somewhat unusual in that her "makeover" was going to be the subject of an article in *Elle* magazine, where Laurie was then managing editor. The magazine was doing an entire makeover issue, and since Laurie was ready to redecorate in any case, she decided to have Use What You Have® redo her living and dining rooms so that she could then write about the experience. Her colleagues, she told me, were very fashion forward, and she'd always doubted that her home reflected her own sense of style. A willowy blonde with a true natural beauty, she just wanted the house where she lived with her husband and three-year-old daughter, Edie, to say "This is my home, and it really shows who I am today."

The Diagnosis
THE LIVING ROOM

The couple lives in a two-story home whose ground floor opens through two double French doors to a garden. The dining room is at the front of the house, and the living room beyond is a step up and separated from the dining

The arrangement of the furniture blocks the natural flow into and around the room—poor feng shui that can be easily remedied.

Before ▼

area by four white columns. The furnishings are eclectic, but all the major wood pieces are old and go well together. Laurie does have sophisticated taste, but her home, while comfortable and attractive, lacked balance.

The sofa was set with its back to the columns and facing the French doors that led out to the garden. Behind it was a long, low, glass-fronted bookcase with a framed wedding photo, a few accessories, and books on top. The columns, the step up to the living area, and the poor furniture placement all effectively blocked an easy flow into the room—very bad feng shui. The sofa was flanked by a standing lamp at one end and an end table with a revolving display of family photos on top at the other. A patterned rug lay in front of the sofa. A small armchair to the right of the rug was angled toward the sofa.

On the right-hand wall, perpendicular to the French doors and the sofa, were a standing torchiere lamp and a tall, glass-fronted breakfront with two small prints hung to the right of it. In the corner to the right of the French doors was an armchair facing toward

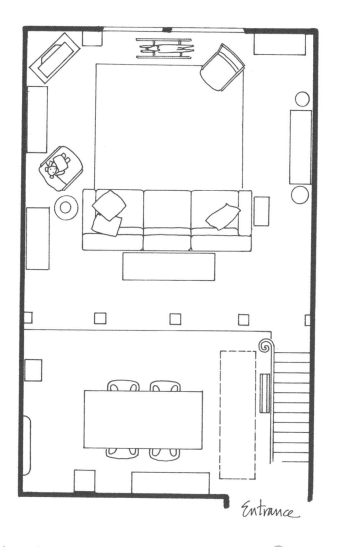

Entrance

Before

the sofa and behind it a small trunk with a very large abstract oil painting hanging above it. A rocking horse was centered directly in front of the left-hand glass door.

In the left-hand corner was a TV in a cabinet set catty-corner and flanked

13

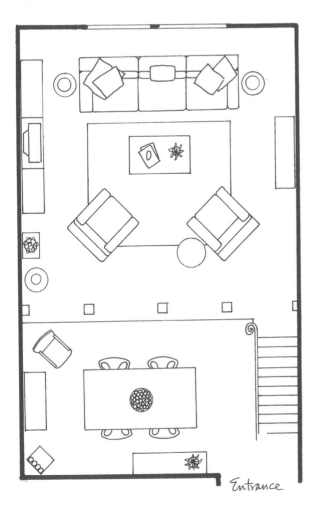

Entrance

After

less in front of the TV and bookcases, at right angles to the sofa.

Farther along the wall, there was a closed cabinet on legs with another large abstract painting over it. In the open space beneath the cabinet there were two baskets filled with Laurie's daughter's toys.

Living Room Mistakes

- Poor furniture placement
- Uncomfortable conversation area
- Lack of balance
- Improper use of artwork
- Ineffective use of accessories
- Awkward traffic pattern

The Remedy

The first thing we did was to turn the sofa around and move it to the far end of the room, with its back to the glass doors. This immediately opened up the traffic pattern, making it more inviting without blocking access through the French doors to the outdoors. We then moved the trunk, which had been in the right-hand cor-

by bookcases, one the same height as the TV cabinet, the other much smaller. Above the smaller bookcase, on the wall to the left of the French doors, Laurie had hung a large print. There was a second armchair more or

After ▲

From the architectural details to the furnishings, artwork, and accessories, all the elements in the room now work together to reflect the owner's true style.

ner, to sit in front of the sofa as a coffee table. The rocking horse would go upstairs to Edie's room.

We removed the closed storage chest from the left-hand wall to the master bedroom and swung the television cabinet flat against the left wall and flanked by the two bookcases plus another I'd found in a bedroom to create the appearance of a single unit of uniform height. The storage baskets that had been on the floor under the open cabinet are now on the bookshelves, with their contents hidden yet

15

"I never would have thought of that!"

Turning the sofa so that its back was to the glass doors and moving it away from the entrance: "The room looks so open now," Laurie said. "It never occurred to me that the sofa should be put in front of the French doors, but it really makes the view of the garden even more appealing."

easily accessible. We accessorized the unit with colorful pottery pieces that had been scattered throughout the living room and dining room. To its left, farthest from the glass doors, we put the end table with a pretty basket of dried flowers on top and hung above it the large painting of a woman that had been in the dining room. The standing lamp, which had been to the left of the sofa, went next to this new arrangement against the wall.

The glass-fronted breakfront on the right-hand wall went into the dining room to be replaced by the long bookcase that had been behind the sofa. The bookcase, with framed photographs on top and the large, red abstract painting hung above it, nicely balanced the television and bookcases on the opposite wall.

Breaking one of my own rules to make Laurie happy—hanging art on small walls next to windows—we hung three tiny botanical prints that had been in the dining room to the left of the French doors. To balance them, we hung three other small prints on the wall to the right. Fortunately, with the small prints hung vertically, there was still enough wall space on either side of them so that they didn't distract from the view.

The Diagnosis
THE DINING ROOM

The entrance to Laurie's home is through a narrow hall with the dining room opening directly to the left, just past the kitchen. A wrought-iron staircase, on the right wall, leads to the second floor.

On the front wall of the dining area was a bureau with an attached mirror,

▲
Before ▶

which is really a bedroom piece, and, to the right of that, a Victorian bamboo stand holding a vase of flowers. Several prints were hung on the wall above it. The adjacent wall, opposite the staircase, held a bracketed display shelf with some accessories and three decorative plates hung above it, and a large portrait of a woman hanging to the right. A small oak cupboard with a

display of four vintage seltzer bottles on top stood in the corner.

The dining table was covered with a botanical-print cloth and held a pretty wood pedestal bowl with some lady apples in it. The light fixture was an industrial-looking metal hanging lamp that focused the light directly down onto the table.

above right: Out of balance and out of sync, this room will benefit from a little fine-tuning.

above left: None of the beautiful pieces in this dining room is shown to its best advantage.

17

Dining Room Mistakes

- Ineffective use of accessories
- Improper use of artwork
- Poor furniture placement
- Furniture of different heights

The Remedy

In the dining room, we removed the display shelf and used that wall for the tall breakfront from the living room, which we filled with china and serving pieces. It looked very elegant, its height and weight balanced the dining table and chairs, and it was, in any case, more appropriate in its new location than it had been in the living room. I moved the small oak cupboard to stand angled in the corner to the left of the breakfront. One of the small armchairs from the living room was now placed in the corner to the right of the breakfront to be used for extra seating at the dining table. We then removed the mirror from the bureau so that it would be less like a bedroom piece and hung the large yellow abstract painting from the living room slightly off center to balance the height

◀ After

above:
Simple, elegant pieces now work in harmony.

far left: Each piece is shown to its full advantage without distractions.

Gracious, serene, and fluid, the newly
reconfigured space provides an open
traffic pattern.

After ▲

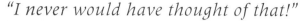

"I never would have thought of that!"

Moving the breakfront from the living room to the dining room: "I was afraid it would be too big for the dining room, but instead of dwarfing it, it really draws your eye to the back wall and makes the room look larger."

and weight of the breakfront on the adjacent wall and bridge the gap between the bureau and the oak cupboard in the corner.

Finally, to give the whole room a cleaner, more elegant look, we removed the tablecloth and left the wooden bowl of apples in the center of the bare table.

Long-Term Recommendations

Although the appearance of both the living and dining rooms was immediately improved, Laurie would have to purchase a few additional items to create a better sense of balance and improve the lighting in the living and dining rooms.

Her most important purchases would be a pair of club chairs the same height as the sofa and a pair of standing lamps to complete the conversation area in the living room as well as to introduce at least two "pairs" into a room that had none.

For the chairs, we tentatively decided on a beautiful plum-brown color picked up from the rug, but I warned Laurie that the color would be difficult to find—as, indeed, it turned out to be. She couldn't find just the right color plum (as much as we both loved it) and opted instead for a stylish pair in chartreuse leather that matched the green in the rug. With the standing lamps and chairs in place, the conversation area was comfortable, complete, and well balanced. A pair of newly purchased green throw pillows for the sofa further accentuated and tied in the green from the rug and the chairs.

In the dining room, Laurie replaced the metal hanging fixture with four halogen spots on a white track that made the room look bigger and brighter and could be adjusted to highlight the dining table, artwork, and accessories.

THE CLIENT'S REACTION

Laurie was delighted to see that her home could so easily appear more stylish—and truly express who she really was—while at the same time be even more practical and functional than it had been before. She told me that she'd had some trepidation about inviting me in because she'd been worried that I'd be "judging" what she'd done (or, more likely, had not done) with her living space, but as we were working together she gleefully acknowledged that she was having a great time. "The process is so intimate," she said, "but it's also really fun."

2

Downsizing Downtown

MOVING TO A SMALLER SPACE

The Client
and the Complaint

"Even though I love the light in this apartment and the rooms have much more character than my last home, I'm stumped about how to make this place function and look good at the same time."

Jeff Adelman is a fun, upbeat kind of guy. He's actually one of the most jovial people I've ever met, always laughing and smiling, but when I went to see him in his new home, he needed some serious help even though he was excited about the move. He was downsizing from a postmodern one-

Jeffry Adelman

Starting with a blank slate can be as exhilarating as it is intimidating, especially when a room needs to be multipurpose. But this nicely proportioned space had lots of potential; it just had to be imagined.

bedroom apartment on the Upper East Side to a smaller one-bedroom in a landmarked building in the Chelsea section of New York City. When I first saw the space it was completely empty.

A sixty-year-old marketing consultant, Jeff was a pioneer in the field of on-line marketing and is presently the CEO of his own consulting firm.

▼ Before ▶

Because he has a home office, he needed to figure out how to create both living and office space that would be stylish, comfortable, and practical in only five hundred square feet. What furniture would he be able to keep? What would he have to discard? What would he need to buy? And how could he create adequate closed storage?

The Diagnosis

The new apartment, in a 1920s building, has nice hardwood floors and two large windows in the main room that let in a lot of light. Just off the main room, separated by French doors, is a small, 8 by 10–foot bedroom, which Jeff had decided to use as his office. Because of that he would, in effect, be *living* in a single room.

As it turned out, he already had al-most all the furniture he needed. (I had worked with Jeff before and knew not only his taste and style but also what furnishings and accessories he already owned.) His Vico Magistretti dining table with a tripod wooden base and round glass top would work well

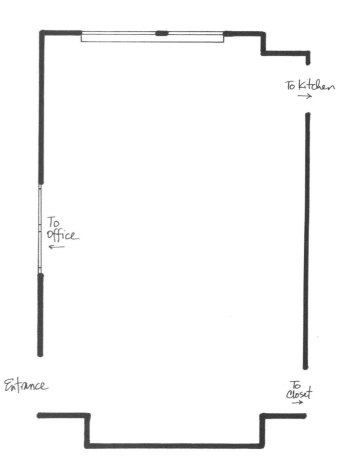

Before

in his new space if he cut down the top from 58 inches to 38 inches. He could use just two of the four Eames dining chairs on a daily basis, keeping the re-maining two in a closet until he had guests.

He'd be able to use the modern sofa, which was upholstered in navy velvet, and a couple of comfortable gray slipper chairs that had been in his previous apartment. He also had a small, hammered-metal Indian table that he could use as a cocktail table. Jeff also had an impressive collection of contemporary black-and-white photographs that would require some careful thought in displaying them to best advantage in this small area. Finally, one of the keys to making his new living space as functional as he wanted it would be to incorporate as much closed storage as possible.

The Remedy

Since Jeff's apartment was totally unfurnished on the day of my initial visit, it was important that I help him to determine how best to arrange the furniture he'd be bringing with him as well as what he would need to buy or have built.

The sofa would go on the long wall opposite the entrance, between the door to the kitchen and the door to the

at right: Most of Jeffry's furniture and accessories from his previous home were put to good use in this highly functional and sophisticated room.

After ▶

26

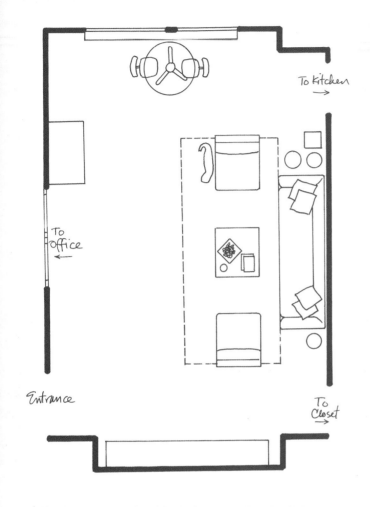

To Kitchen →

To Office ←

Entrance

To Closet →

After

chor the space without making it appear even smaller.

Given the lack of available wall space, I advised him to purchase or to have built a long white shelf to go over the sofa as a flexible display space for his photographs. Not only would this create a dramatic focal point for the room, but it would also allow him to rotate the exhibit, since he had more photographs than could be displayed at one time.

The dining table and chairs would go under the windows, and the television, which was in an enclosed case on wheels, would be placed to the right of French doors leading to the office, opposite the sofa. For storage, I suggested that he eventually get two long cabinets on casters in black painted wood or mica that could slide under the window frames and would provide extra surface area when he entertained or needed more work space.

For lighting, I recommended that he have a track installed between the ceiling beams with five tiny halogen spots to provide general illumination and also that he purchase two pharmacy lamps that he could place next to

closet, with his two slipper chairs at either end to create a U shape. The Indian table, placed in the center, would complete the conversation area, and a neutral-colored sisal rug, which he would have to purchase, would an-

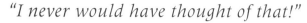

"I never would have thought of that!"

Cutting down the glass top of the dining table: "I have to admit I had my doubts about how the scale of the smaller glass top would look with the base," Jeff admitted, "but I'm thrilled! It still looks good and the expense was minimal."

two black, steel, or green postmodern end tables at either end of the sofa.

Pleated window shades that opened from either the top or the bottom would allow him to drop the top for privacy, if he wished, without blocking the light or his view of the sky.

Jeff had already seen a mirrored Murphy bed that he wanted to purchase for the wall opposite the windows. I agreed that the hidden bed would be a good idea, but suggested something without mirrored doors, which might be more of a distraction rather than an aid in enlarging the room.

Finally, if he found that he needed even more storage space, he could have another small, low unit built to go next to the television cabinet on the wall between the windows and the French doors to the office.

The Ultimate Result

When I returned to Jeff's apartment several months later, it had truly been transformed, and he was delighted with the way it had turned out. "I'm not alone when I say I think I have the nicest studio I've ever seen," he told me. "Other people have said the same thing."

The cut-down dining table top and two chairs fit beautifully in front of the windows, and the sofa and chairs were in place along with the hammered metal coffee table. Although he'd decided against the end tables, he did purchase two Jasper Morrison Luxmaster floor lamps for either end of the sofa, which was accented with silk throw pillows in saffron orange and yellow.

Instead of the shelf that I'd suggested he have built above the sofa,

he'd opted to hang a striking black-and-white Michael Spano photograph of an old woman sitting on a bench.

The Murphy bed he'd ultimately chosen was made of white wood with closed storage on either side. When it's closed, the bed unit virtually disappears into the wall opposite the windows, and to open it, all he has to do is move aside one of the slipper chairs. When it's open, there's a copy of a photograph of a Buddhist monk taken by Chan Chao above the bed, two small orange reading lights of Italian design in addition to built-in halogen spots above the "headboard," pillows that coordinate with those on the sofa, and a pea-green quilted coverlet that he uses as a spread. All in all, it's both functional and aesthetically pleasing.

While I was there, I helped him arrange some of his accessories. On the coffee table we placed a 150-year-old Sri Lankan Buddha, along with a vase of tulips on a small, square silver tray and an orange-colored 1950s Venetian glass apple. On top of the television, we arranged a display of colorful glass vases.

After ▶

at right: This dramatic and elegantly accessorized sleeping area virtually disappears into the wall when not in use.

30

Jeff also had several late-nineteenth-century wooden animal sculptures from Guatemala, which we grouped in the corner between the dining table and the television. The only exception was a large cat with a movable head and tail, which we placed next to the slipper chair nearest the windows as a kind of mascot.

THE CLIENT'S REACTION

Things really fit into this space. The way things look is very important to me," Jeff remarked. "It's beautiful and peaceful, and it has a calming, comfortable effect on me. And I love the way the living room seating is arranged. Because my hearing is somewhat impaired, the proximity of the chairs to the sofa makes it really easy for me to have a conversation without straining to hear what people are saying.

"I like this place much better than the last," he admitted, "and I used literally everything I had except for my queen-size bed and one bookcase. It's amazing!"

3

Home Alone!

LIFE AFTER ROOMMATES

The Client
and the Complaint

"I think I'm in a period of self-discovery and renewal," said George Alexander when we discussed my coming to help him with his apart-ment. "Now it's time for the space to reflect me and not other people."

In fact, George had been sharing his living space with "other people" for much of the last decade. He came to New York from his native Alabama to attend Columbia Business School, and after receiving his MBA he began his career in banking. About ten years ago he found the apartment in which he is

George Alexander, now free of
roommates, was ready to create
a real home for himself.

still living (and where, he says, he fully intends to stay forever). A large, gracious space in a named building on 116th Street and Adam Clayton Powell, Jr. Boulevard, it's approximately 2,400 square feet, with nine rooms, multiple fireplaces, and 10-foot ceilings.

Not long after moving in, however, he realized that he wanted to make a career change. He loved "everything about the movies" and determined to give up banking in order to find his place as a writer and/or director in the film business. To support himself through the transition, he started writing about movies and went to work for HBO, the cable movie network. But he also decided that he would need to take in one or two roommates. The apartment was large, there was certainly plenty of room, and it seemed like a logical way to help defray expenses.

For a time, all went well. The roommates were, as he put it, "low key," and he didn't really feel their presence. As the years went by, however, he was finding it more and more difficult to write at home, particularly since one of his more recent roommates was a classic couch potato who seemed to spend most of his days watching television in the living room. Not only did the noise disturb George when he was trying to work, but he also found it increasingly irritating just to see the guy lying around doing nothing. "I didn't realize what the cost would be to my creativity and independence," he told me when we met. "It wasn't worth it—particularly as a writer. It was mental anguish. I even started to avoid going home and would write in Starbucks. But it taught me what I need and what I was or was not willing to compromise about." One thing he decided was that, as soon as it was financially feasible, the roommates would have to go.

In the course of his writing for HBO, George had interviewed some prominent filmmakers, including actor Forest Whittaker, cinematographer/director Ernest Dickerson, and actress/writer/director Kasi Lemmons. Now he had an idea. Why not write a book about black filmmakers? Serendipitously, through his volunteer work, he met Janet Hill, an editor at Broadway/

Doubleday, and when he described the project to her, her immediate response was "I've always wanted to do that book! Why don't you write it for me?" *Why We Make Movies: Black Filmmakers Talk About the Magic of Cinema* was published in 2003. Since then, George has produced a documentary version of the book, appeared on National Public Radio, and receives invitations to participate in panel discussions and to appear at film festivals. Finally, in June 2004 he became roommate-free, and soon after he realized he was ready to start decorating his home.

The Diagnosis

Finally, George was able to "spread out" and use his entire apartment. He was using one room as a study and another as a storage room, but the room he really wanted to work on was the living room. "This is not showing any creativity or imagination," he said when I arrived. "Things are just here."

Against one long wall stood a sofa upholstered in gold velvet with two

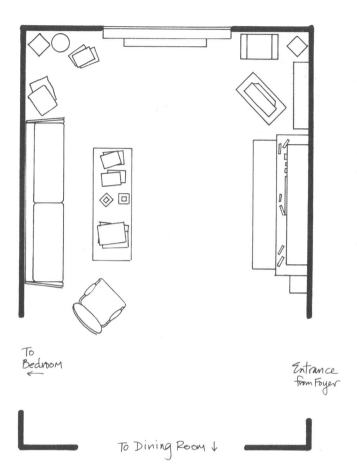

To Bedroom
←

Entrance from Foyer

To Dining Room ↓

Before

black throw pillows on the floor to its right. Perpendicular to the sofa, but angled away from it was a French armchair with a cream striped fabric on the seat, back, and arms. A long wooden bench with various magazines and books on top was serving as a coffee table. Two sconces on the wall

35

above the sofa provided the only lighting on that side of the room.

On the shorter, window wall, perpendicular and to the right of the sofa wall, he'd hung a piece of modern art in a gold-leaf frame. On the floor below it were a stereo speaker and a small, wooden African footstool.

The fireplace is on the long wall directly opposite the sofa. On the mantel, leaning against the wall, was another piece of modern art along with a few family photos in various framing materials and a couple of postcards with a picture of his book. On the wall

◄ Before ▼

above: The fine fireplace, which should have been the focal point of the room, is lost amidst a jumble of distracting bits and pieces.

right: This beautifully proportioned room with fine architectural details had all the makings of a really spectacular space.

above it were two more sconces that provided the only other lighting in the room.

To the left of the fireplace was a large bookcase stacked with CDs and DVDs. And in the corner of the window wall was the second stereo speaker. At this end of the window wall was a white metal stand holding George's audio components, above which hung an African mask. A cart angled in the corner in front of the bookcase held the television, VCR, and cable box.

All in all, the room was spare but functional. There was, however, no real conversation area, and while the bench worked as a coffee table the whole arrangement didn't really hang together as well as it could have.

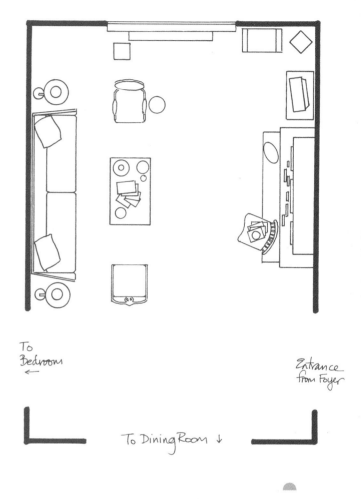

After

The Mistakes

- Uncomfortable conversation area
- Poor furniture placement
- Badly lit room
- Ignoring the focal point
- Lack of balance
- Lack of cohesion
- Improper use of artwork
- Ineffective use of accessories

The Remedy

The first thing I did was to look around the rest of the apartment to see if there were any hidden treasures we could use to give the living room a more pulled-together look and get George to

37

the next level, as he wanted. And, sure enough, it turned out that he had more than he knew.

I found a standing lamp in the bedroom and, happily, its mate in the study. Reunited, they now flank the sofa, providing both more light and more balance. Also in the bedroom I found an antique wooden trunk that George told me he'd gotten at an auction house along with the sofa and the French armchair. I thought they belonged together and moved the trunk into the living room to replace the bench he'd been using as a coffee table. (The bench went into the foyer, where he could use it to put things down or remove his boots when he came into the house.) Then, we moved the French armchair from the left to the right end of the sofa and brought in a black wooden chair from the dining room to complete the U-shaped conversation area at least temporarily. Next to the armchair we placed the African footstool and accessorized it with a small candelabra and a little African drum.

at right: Creating a well-balanced and useful conversation area is only the beginning of this room's transformation.

After ▶

On top of the coffee table we collected three Mexican pots that brought back warm memories of vacations he'd spent there (and incidentally picked up the gold color in the sofa fabric), along with a few of his favorite books, a playbill from the original production of *A Raisin in the Sun*, and a sand dollar he'd also found on the beach in Mexico.

To the right of the fireplace hearth, we placed a small cherrywood bench that had been in the hallway and

Not only are the artwork and accessories well showcased, but also the fireplace now commands the attention that it deserves.

▲
After ▶

Every home should reflect the taste and interests of its owner. Here, a collection of books, memorabilia, and artifacts from George's travels makes an appealing and personalized statement.

"I never would have thought of that!"

Arranging the Mexican paintings and the photos on the mantel: "It feels great to have those paintings together where I can see them," he said. "I didn't see them before, and it brings out the character of the room having the pair together."

stacked it with a few more books, topped by a hula doll for fun and a couple of bananas to create an amusing vignette and a yellow accent. On the other side of the hearth, to balance the bench, we brought in a carved African fertility sculpture that had been lost in the dining room. (George later told me that the sculpture, African mask, and a couple of other pieces were given to him in lieu of rent by one of his roommates who'd been collecting African art.)

On the fireplace mantel we placed two Mexican watercolors in matching frames (one of which had been in the dining room and the other in the study) flanking a mirror I'd found in the bedroom hallway that balanced the height of the sconces. We finished the arrangement with a few old, black-

and-white family photographs, and I suggested that if George gathered more photos, he could expand the vignette.

In the dining room, I found a small oak chest that had been discarded by a neighbor. We removed the large bookcase from the wall to the left of the fireplace and put the chest in its place, with the TV on top and all the CDs and DVDs stored inside. The TV cart could then be used for the audio equipment, and the white metal piece, which was really meant to be outdoor furniture, could be discarded. Now there is no tall bookcase to create a roller-coaster effect on that wall, and all the tapes are neatly stored out of sight.

Finally, we put the pair of black throw pillows at either end of the sofa instead of on the floor, and above it,

41

between the sconces, we hung two more pieces of African art acquired from the now-departed roommate.

Long-Term Recommendations

Since the walls were in need of a fresh coat of paint, I suggested that he have them painted in a pale banana or linen color. For the windows, I recommended bamboo matchstick blinds hung inside the frames and, to anchor the conversation area, a dark blue or green sisal rug that would pick up the colors in the Mexican pottery on the coffee table.

Since George seemed to be so good at finding things in auction houses (not to mention his neighbor's discard pile), I suggested that, in his travels, he try to find a second French armchair to replace the wooden armless one I'd brought from the dining room and that he then have the two reupholstered in matching fabric. He could also be on the lookout for different, more dramatic antique sconces to replace the ones above the sofa and the mantel. And finally, to give him even better light, he could increase the wattage in the floor lamps by having them rewired for three-way bulbs.

THE CLIENT'S REACTION

This really makes me feel more adult. It reflects different periods in my life and celebrates things that are important to me," George declared. "Before it felt like a dorm without personality; now it feels like a real lounge. It feels like the space is sacred. Use What You Have® really does work."

4

Furniture the Size of Texas

ACCOMMODATING A TRANSFER

The Clients and the Complaint

"I wanted to use as much of what we had as possible, and when I heard the name of your company, I thought that said it all," Gerald Balboa told me when I arrived at the gracious 1,600-square-foot apartment he and his family had just moved into from their much larger Houston home. "The architecture here is unusual," he went on. "Things sort of stick out, and the biggest problem for me, coming from Texas, is that I want to keep an open feeling."

Gerald and Olga, both in their thirties, are native Texans who met in

Olga, Gerald, and Christina Balboa

graduate school. They moved to New York when his company transferred him. Olga, a petite, long-haired attorney with a bright smile, is now a stay-at-home mom taking care of their ten-month-old daughter, Christina. And when Gerald told me they were somewhat overwhelmed by the problem of fitting their Texas-style furniture into this much smaller space, he wasn't overstating their dilemma.

The Diagnosis

The Balboas' furniture had arrived shortly before our consultation. Gerald told me that they'd already divested themselves of almost half of what they'd had, but what was left was BIG. They had a large sofa, an oversized chair and matching ottoman, a *huge* coffee table, three 7-foot-tall dark wood bookcases, a tall, dark-wood armoire,

Before ▼

Texas-sized furniture was having a hard time fitting into a smaller space in New York City.

a couple of smaller end tables, and a 36-inch Sony television that had been in the family room back in Texas.

Not only was everything big, but also the living room was a different shape from the one they'd had previously, in addition to which it did have several jogs in the corners—things sticking out—as Gerald had noted. I could see why they were worried about fitting it all in and still having open space for the baby to crawl around.

▶ When you walk in the front door, there is a wall directly ahead and just 8 feet in front of you. The bedrooms are to the left, and straight to the right is the living room. Once you enter the living room, the dining room is to the left, accessible from both the living room and the kitchen, and the large living room window with a Juliet balcony on either side is directly opposite you. The layout is, in fact, very gracious, and the living room is quite large: 22 by 18 feet.

The sofa was on the wall opposite the dining room, and although the Balboas weren't certain it worked in

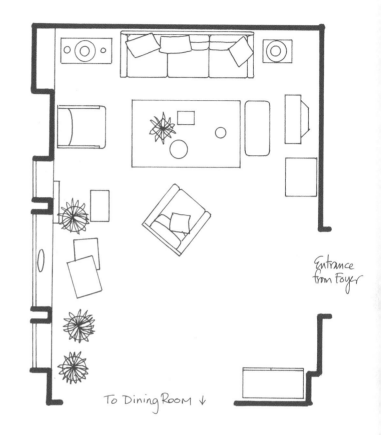

Entrance from Foyer

To Dining Room ↓

Before

that position, I liked it very much and thought they would, too, after we'd made other changes. The sofa was flanked by a small mahogany end table with a lamp and a much taller and wider end table of the same wood but a totally different style, holding a matching lamp. Next to the large table, in the corner, one of the bookcases

45

held a collection of autographed footballs framed in Lucite, photographs in various framing materials, and a few pieces of sculpture—in other words, a hodgepodge of objects.

The large television was to the right, on the entrance wall, with a mahogany end table to its right. In front of the television, pushed up against one end of the coffee table, was a very large ottoman, and across from it, completing the U shape, was a deep wooden armchair that Olga said wasn't very comfortable. Across from the sofa, angled toward the television, was yet another chair—actually a chair-and-a-half—that matched the ottoman. The coffee table that completed the conversation area was not only over-sized, it also had many small drawers, which Olga liked because of the storage space they provided but which I was afraid might be dangerous for a crawling baby or toddler.

And finally, immediately to the left of the entrance, on a small wall next to the opening to the dining room, stood the armoire because, in fact, there simply wasn't any other place to put it.

The Mistakes

- Improper furniture placement
- Uncomfortable conversation area
- Lack of cohesion
- Ineffective use of accessories
- Lack of focal point

The Remedy

The Balboas had told me they were planning to buy a rug for the living room, but I was concerned that putting a fine rug in the room where the baby would be playing on the floor might be a mistake. Instead, I suggested they bring in the one they were now using in the dining room, where it was practically hidden under the table in any case. (I believe that rugs are generally troublesome crumb-catchers in frequently used dining rooms, so it seemed like the perfect solution.)

I also suggested that we put the rug on an angle so that one point would be under the center of the sofa with the opposite point coming out into the room. Not only would it be more visible and look more interesting in that position, but the point would provide a nice little soft spot where the baby could sit and play. I could tell by the looks on their faces that they thought I was a little bit crazy, but they agreed to try it, and when we got done, they were happily amazed by how well it worked.

Once the rug was in place, we moved the chair-and-a-half to the right of the sofa, on one of the points of the rug with the ottoman opposite it on the left. We placed the two mahogany end tables of similar height at either end of the sofa. The matching lamps went on top of them. As it happened, the larger table that had been to the left of the sofa has a lovely lyre-shaped base, and when we centered it under the windows with a small lamp, a formal clock, a small bronze sculpture of blind justice, and a flower arrangement in a burgundy porcelain and brass-footed bowl, it really showed off the piece and created a secondary focal point.

In front of the left-hand Juliet balcony door beside the lyre-based table, we angled the wooden armchair with a tree standing behind it. The fact that the chair isn't very comfortable will be

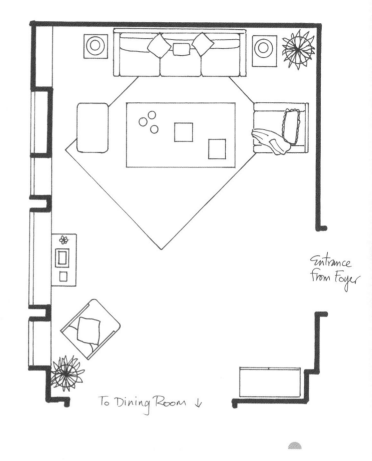

Entrance from Foyer

To Dining Room ↓

After

less of a problem since it's not part of the main conversation area and won't get used as much.

The large television remained an issue, but the Balboas told me that in their previous home the armoire had housed a smaller television so we moved the Sony into the armoire and adjusted the hole in the back to fit the larger television and cable wires. Since

After ▲

Using pairs effectively and balancing tall pieces gives this room a well-ordered look without feeling stodgy.

far right: This beautiful table with its lyre-shaped base is shown off when appropriately positioned and decorated with well-chosen accessories.

the armoire is in a good position for viewing from the seating area, another problem was solved.

I found a round mirror in a gold-leaf frame and several botanical prints that had not yet been rehung since the move. We centered the mirror on the wall over the sofa with two of the prints, one on either side, to create a focal point that is more dramatic than that of the windows.

To finish off the new arrangement, we accessorized the coffee table with a couple of pretty wooden boxes, an orchid plant, and three brass candlesticks.

Long-Term Recommendations

Since Olga and Gerald didn't know how long they'd be staying in their new home—it would depend on

After ▲

"I never would have thought of that!"

Putting the rug on an angle and leaving the furniture straight: The Balboas were skeptical that this would work, but after seeing how it not only adds visual interest to the room but also makes the furniture arrangement seem less boxy, they were convinced.

whether or not Gerald was transferred again—they were reluctant to invest too much in things that couldn't be moved.

I did, however, suggest that they purchase pleated shades to hang inside the frames of the windows in the living room and the dining room as well as the doors to the balconies to give them more privacy. Because the windows are all "tilt and turn" and they, along with the balcony doors, open in, there would be no way for them to hang curtains.

I recommended that they buy a second end table to match the square one we'd placed next to the sofa so that they'd have an additional pair to provide a stronger sense of balance. And I thought that if they needed more light, they could buy a dark metal pharmacy lamp to stand to the right side of the club chair.

I also urged Olga to consider replacing the large coffee table with a smaller, oval one. It could have shelves below to hold magazines and newspapers, but it wouldn't take up so much space and the room would feel even more open. Eliminating sharp corners and drawers would make the place safer for an active child.

The bookcase could be used as a kind of gallery for family photographs. We immediately arranged all those photos in silver-toned frames, and Olga said that she would reframe the others. If she wanted, she could also use the bottom shelf for photo albums, which I recommended she have bound in matching burgundy or gold-colored leather.

THE CLIENTS' REACTION

We'd both been a bit overwhelmed by our cross-country move to a new city with a young baby," said Olga. "We are so relieved to have our things organized now. It's looking like a home."

"Everything still feels so open, and it looks so much better than we expected," Gerald echoed. "I can't believe it's so elegant."

5

Clearing the Clutter

COMING TO TERMS WITH AN OVERSTUFFED HOME

Bailey Beeken and David
Wilkie, with son, Beau
(on coffee table), and
daughter, Quinn

The Clients and the Complaint

"Lauri, *help*! Not only has our family grown, but so has our stuff. Even though we have more space now than we did when we worked with you in our last place, we're overwhelmed, and we need you to come help us again as soon as possible." That was what one of my clients said when she called to set up an appointment.

Bailey Beeken is the director of trade shows and conferences for a media company while her husband, David Wilkie, is a video editor and

Before ▲

A lot of furniture, accessories, and artwork—a growing family's stuff—was overwhelming them.

producer of documentaries who works from home. I'd first met the couple several years ago, when they called me in to clear the clutter in their previous home. Since then, they'd become parents of two children, Beau, five, and Quinn, four, and had moved to a larger home. But because they were both busy with careers and raising their family, they didn't have much energy left for pulling it together. They'd been living in their "new" space for a couple of years, and the clutter had once more caught up with them.

The Diagnosis

There was so much stuff in the living room that even I was a bit overwhelmed. Although I'd arrived with a group of eight trainees, I was afraid we would not be able to move all the furniture without calling on the Santini Brothers for assistance. But the clients wanted it fixed that day!

Against the right wall there was a large L-shaped sofa with the back of the L facing the entrance and obstructing the flow of traffic into the room. A rocking chair placed with its back to the window faced the sofa, but there was no coffee table to hold the conversation area together. In the corner, next to the rocking chair, was a small stone-topped white cabinet serving as a base for a lamp and a couple of framed photos. Next to the sofa, along the same wall and closer to the entrance, were a standing lamp and then a row of tall bookcases. The shelves were filled haphazardly with books and topped with a hodgepodge of objects. Four of the couple's six guitars hung down in front of them. (The other two were in cases on the floor.) Behind the L of the sofa, they had placed a "desk" made from a large slab of marble on two wooden bedside tables. An old wooden, swivel desk chair

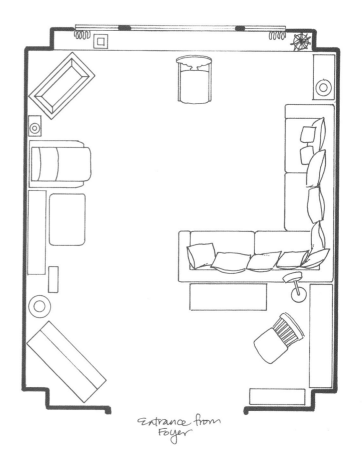

Entrance from
Foyer

Before

53

Before ▲

This room lacked balance and function, both of which could be achieved with some simple moves.

stood in front of the bookcases close to the desk.

The entranceway was flanked to the right by another small white cabinet with a stone top and a rolltop desk set catty-corner to the left. From there, marching along the left-hand wall toward the window wall was a standing lamp, a tall, narrow bookcase, a music stand, two low bookcases with an ottoman in front, a Morris chair, a small wooden table with a lamp, and a large dollhouse, which actually served as a cabinet for the television. Another small lamp was placed on the window ledge.

Artwork was hung haphazardly on all the walls. Accessories and collectibles occupied virtually every surface. It seemed that almost nothing in that room was working.

The Mistakes

- Improper furniture placement
- Uncomfortable conversation area
- Poor traffic pattern
- Furniture of different heights
- Lack of balance
- Lack of cohesion
- Inadequate lighting
- Improper use of artwork
- Ineffective use of accessories

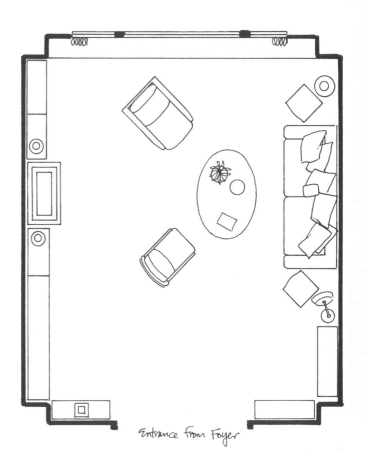

Entrance from Foyer

After

The Remedy

The first thing we did was to take almost *everything* out of the room in order to determine what to keep and what to banish.

We decided not to put back the L section of the sofa, because that configuration creates the most uncomfortable seating area, causing anyone trying to carry on a conversation to have to "twist and shout"—like the

55

Judicious editing and placement
helped to create a comfortable and
accessible conversation area.

▲ After

Beatles' song. So the L part of the sofa would be moved either into the bedroom as a loveseat or into the children's playroom. The pair of bedside tables that had been serving as a base for the marble-topped desk became end tables for the sofa, and the two standing lamps were then moved to become task lighting at either end of the sofa. The rocking chair was set on an angle perpendicular to the sofa, at the end of the room closest to the entrance, while the Morris chair completed the comfortable U-shaped conversation area at the window end of the room. I found an oval coffee table pushed against the wall of a bedroom and brought it in to complete the arrangement. An interesting darkwood cabinet that complemented the sofa and the rocker was moved from the foyer to the wall where the tall bookcases had been to serve as both storage and display space. The result was a much more comfortable conversation area, improved lighting, and a better traffic pattern, as well as more cohesion and better balance in the room.

On the wall above the sofa, we hung a very nice, 24 by 36–inch wood-framed mirror that had been in the entrance hall and balanced it with four beautiful, similarly framed Japanese woodblock prints that had been scattered in various places throughout the home. The result was a well-designed secondary focal point (the view being the primary one), with space for the eye to rest on either side. To highlight the prints even more, we gathered all the best throw pillows from around the room and arranged them on the sofa, with their points turned upward.

The tall bookcases, which had been displaced from the sofa wall, were really several low pieces that had been piled on top of one another. We broke them down and lined them up along the left wall, with the dollhouse/TV cabinet centered between them to break up the space. We then turned the tall, narrow wooden bookcase on its side and positioned it across the top of the other bookcases, filling the now-horizontal open niches with CDs instead of books. Above, we hung two groups of three guitars, all at the same

"I never would have thought of that!"

Creating a "media wall" by centering the dollhouse/TV cabinet across from the sofa and balancing it with the books, guitars, and CDs on either side.

height. The small table lamp that had been in the right-hand corner near the windows was reunited with its mate, which had been in the bedroom, and we set them on either side of the dollhouse for balance. The result? No more roller-coaster effect from furniture of different heights, books and CDs that are much more accessible, and an interesting tertiary focal point created by the hanging guitars. In addition, the television, which is hidden in the dollhouse, is easier to see from anywhere in the conversation area.

To complete the new look, we placed a couple of pieces of pretty pottery on the end table closest to the window; gathered a metalwork box,

Innovation was the key to creating appropriate storage and display space for extensive CD and guitar collections.

After ▶

58

an old match-striker, a piece of art deco sculpture, and an orchid plant to create a display on the coffee table; and set a large piece of pottery along with an arrangement of flowers on the small white cabinet near the windows. Because the clients wanted to keep the plants that had been scattered around the room, we collected them all on top of the dollhouse to create a cohesive "rooftop garden" display.

Long-Term Recommendations

Although the improvements we were able to make in a single day were quite dramatic and the clients were extremely pleased with the immediate result, there was much to be done to complete the transformation.

The room needed painting, and I recommended that they have it done in the same sand color as the kitchen, with the portion of the wall above the picture molding in an eggshell finish of the same color rather than white, as it is now, so that the line would remain unbroken and the eye would continue to travel upward to the ceiling.

The sofa, which was covered in a light-colored fabric, was quite worn, and they were thinking of replacing it in the next year or so. I suggested that, when they did that, they buy one covered in neutral-colored rayon chenille, which would be both durable and comfortable. To finish the conversation area properly, I also recommended that they purchase a pair of upholstered chairs the same height as the new sofa, in a durable woven or nubby fabric, or in leather, that would be more comfortable than the wooden-armed rocker and Morris chair, both of which could be moved into either the children's room or the master bedroom. The rug was a neutral color and in relatively good condition, although worn in some spots. I suggested that, for the time being, they buy new padding, which would help to even out the worn spots, and that when they were ready for a new rug, they stick with a neutral color that would tie in with the neutrals they already had. The coffee table, which had a lovely marquetry top, was in need of some repair, and they said that they would have it fixed.

Because the bedside tables, which had been used to make the "desk" and were now being used as end tables, are rather small, I suggested they eventually be replaced with a pair of larger tables. They could also purchase a pair of hammered-metal table lamps to replace the standing lamps at either end of the sofa. If they did that, the standing lamp closest to the windows could move across to the corner on the left side of the room.

With the new end tables, the bedside tables could once again be used to support a desk top, but the marble top would be replaced with a wooden one stained to match the bedside tables and the tables could be raised on metal casters so that the desk would be a more comfortable height. This new "desk" could be set against the far right wall, parallel to the windows. The old wooden chair could be replaced with a smaller, black, armless desk chair that

would take up less space and could be tucked neatly under the desk when not in use.

To transform the window treatment I recommended removing the patterned curtains and replacing them with pleated shades that could be pulled down from the top for privacy without blocking the view. If they wanted to, they could have a 7 to 8–foot cornice made and upholstered in a fabric to complement the sofa and chairs. Then, for an even more cohesive look, they could have two 18-inch pillows made in the same fabric to put on the sofa and matching cushions for the wide windowsill to create a comfortable window seat.

The bookcases needed to be repainted in one color so that they all matched, with the books rearranged so that their heights were consistent. The tops of the cases should remain bare so that the clutter wouldn't detract from the guitars hanging on the wall above them.

THE CLIENTS' REACTION

It's really amazing," Bailey said, "how tranquil the room feels now. And that's very important to us at this stage of our lives. We still have all the things we love—our artwork, our books, and our music—only the clutter is gone. This is exactly what we needed, and we know it's going to look even better when we finish. It will be great to be able just to sit here and relax."

Serviceable and Stylish

CREATING A HOME OFFICE

Olivia and Bill Blumer

The Clients and the Complaint

"We put this office together quickly, and it wasn't right or attractive," Olivia (Liv) Blumer said as she led me into the room. "We know it can work better, but because we're not sure how long we're going to be staying here, we don't want to invest a lot. Aside from the fact that it has functional problems, it also looks like hell," she concluded, with her characteristic candor.

Liv Blumer is a literary agent who had recently set up her own shop, along with her husband, Bill, who had worked in advertising and marketing research for many years. He had opened his own home-based business fifteen years earlier and already had his own office in the spacious home where they'd been living with several generations of cats for about twenty-eight years.

"Bill and I have been together since we met as kids in summer camp, and we have a great working relationship, but now I also need a room of my own," Liv explained. "The room I'm using as an office used to be our guest room, and I also used the desk to pay bills and write thank-you notes. It had been that way for so long that we really couldn't see it anymore," she went on. "And now that we have our own business, we've been too busy working to do anything about it. It doesn't have great storage, we need a library, and we need someplace to hold a meeting comfortably without invading our living space."

The hastily put together work-at-home space in a former guest bedroom was neither optimally functional nor attractive.

Before ▶

The Diagnosis

As is usually the case, Liv was astute enough to have hit the nail right on the head, even though she couldn't quite see how to solve the problem she'd identified.

The problem was, indeed, partly aesthetic, but it was also very much related to function. Liv's desk, a mahogany empire table that had belonged to her grandmother, was placed perpendicular to the two windows at the far end of the room. Next to it sat a brown metal file cabinet. Then, on the wall behind her were three more file cabinets—two beige, one black—and across the top of the beige ones she'd placed a piece of mica to form a work surface on which she had her computer. (Liv told me that she and Bill had found the two beige files on the street. "We're great little street pickers, and proud of it," she said gleefully.) The trouble with this arrangement was that she had to swing completely around in her chair to move from the desk to the computer and back.

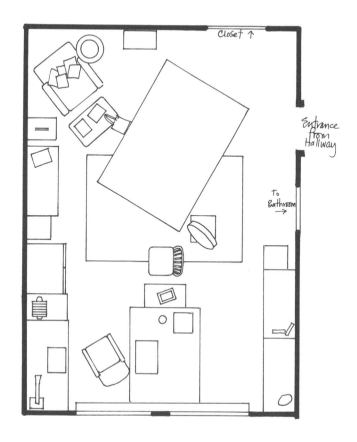

Next to the black file, which was farthest from the window, was another closed wooden cabinet, and, on the opposite wall—so that she had to get up and walk around it to reach them—were two bookcases, painted the same attractive spring green as the walls but of different heights and with a lot of wasted space above them.

Before

65

Something old, something new, something borrowed might spell good luck for a bride, but in this case, they created a catchall corner in what should have been a cozy reading area.

Before ▲

In addition to these "office" pieces, farther down on the same long wall holding the files, was a lovely pecan-wood chest that had also belonged to Liv's grandmother, on top of which was an assortment of manuscripts and papers.

In the corner opposite the door to the room, next to the pecan-wood chest, Liv and Bill had placed a comfortable armchair upholstered in tobacco-colored leather that he had found at a going-out-of-business sale. Next to that was a bronze and cloisonné standing lamp with its original

parchment shade, which had also belonged to Liv's grandmother.

The nice hardwood floors were covered with two oriental rugs, one angled on top of the other for no apparent reason.

On the wall above the leather chair they'd hung a Paul Narkievic print with lots of blues and greens that went well with the walls, while the wood frame complemented the tones of the chest, the chair, and the lamp. On the wall above the workstation, there was a large lavender-blue modern print, and between the two windows, two small pedestals, the upper one holding a harlequin figurine, the lower one a family photograph.

All in all, the room reflected the fact that it had been, by Liv's own admission, pretty much "thrown together." It lacked cohesion from both a practical and an aesthetic point of view.

The Mistakes

- Lack of cohesion
- Awkward traffic pattern
- Lack of focal point
- Uncomfortable (or nonexistent) conversation area

- Poor furniture placement
- Improper use of artwork
- Ineffective use of accessories

The Remedy

At the end of our first meeting I gave Liv and Bill a written design plan. The first order of business (so to speak) was to give Liv a more comfortable work area. I suggested that she paint all the file cabinets black so that they matched one another and pull one of them out from the wall to create an L-shaped work area with another piece of mica cut to match the one she already had. Her chair would be on the inside of the L, with her back to the window. This configuration would be more work-able and allow her unobstructed access to the bookcases on the opposite wall. It would also enable her to give away the single painted wood cabinet, which she would no longer need.

As for the bookcases themselves, I suggested that she replace the two low units she had with a triple built-in case going from the floor almost to the ceil-ing and paint it green to blend with

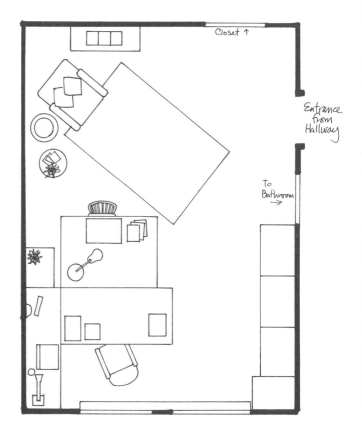

After

the walls. Not only would the shelving then be uniform, but also it would provide a great deal more storage for both books and manuscripts than the shorter ones had.

To create a meeting area, I sug-gested that she and Bill move the Empire table so that its back abutted the far side of the desk and place the

A simple rearrangement of the furniture
that was already in the room makes this
space far more useful and appealing.

After ▲

fourth file cabinet to its right, forming a kind of partner's desk. By putting the green-painted Windsor chair (which was, at the time, serving as a guest chair to the side of her desk) behind it, she could comfortably have a meeting with Bill or a client, and they would both have a place to sit and a surface to write on. In addition, from an aesthetic perspective, the desk is a beautiful piece of furniture that would catch the eye as one entered the room.

At the other end of the room, I suggested that they move the pecan-wood chest from the long wall to the short wall opposite the windows. The chair would remain in its corner, and the lamp would move to its left, where it would be out of the traffic pattern. Then she and Bill could move the Paul Narkievic print so that it hung directly above the chest instead of "floating" where it had been between the chest and the chair. To complete a cozy

After ▲ This corner is now a comfortable refuge for reading, which is a big part of Liv Blumer's job.

reading area, I suggested she bring in a Victorian plant stand (another of Grandmother's treasures) from the living room to serve as a pull-up table and provide a resting place for a book,

"I never would have thought of that!"

Painting all the file cabinets uniformly black: "It seems pretty obvious now," Liv said, "but I never would have thought of it." And putting the desk and the table together "partner style": "Now Liv and I have a place to brainstorm together," Bill commented.

a cup, or a glass. In addition, she could arrange her "in" and "out" boxes of manuscripts and papers neatly on top of the chest. With those changes in place, if two people needed to talk informally, one could sit in the armchair while the other turned around the wooden chair from the partner's desk so that they could chat without shouting from one end of the room to the other.

To create a cleaner, safer, less choppy look and a well-defined traffic pattern, I recommended that they remove the top rug and angle the larger bottom one so that one short end was under the leather chair and the rug itself was on an angle that led you across the floor to the bookcases and the open end of the desk near the windows.

Finally, I suggested that they remove the two small pedestals from the wall between the windows and hang them next to the print above the workstation with two pieces of orange Depression glass I found in another room to pick up the colors in the room and provide a nice contrast to the green walls. Grouping the pedestals with the lavender-blue print would also make the entire arrangement a more effective focal point.

When I returned a few months later, Liv and Bill had completed the plan. The changes have transformed the entire dynamic of the room, making it much more flexible and functional as well as more cohesive and attractive.

THE CLIENTS' REACTION

Before it was a jumble," Bill said. "Now you can see there's lots of open space. It looks bigger and better, it works better, and it's easier to work in."

"We didn't realize we needed a meeting space outside of our living space until now," Liv added. "Everything hangs together *astonishingly* well, and we did this without spending gobs of money."

7

Lost in Translation

SWITCHING FROM RENTING TO OWNING

The Client
and the Complaint

"I love my trees and I love my view," Bonnie Conklin exclaimed as I entered her newly purchased home. "I know I could be happy if I could just get this right, but I'm so busy with my work that I really don't have the time, and even if I did, I really have no idea how to make it look good."

A transplanted Californian in her early fifties, Bonnie, who is the assistant to the president of a major New York cultural institution, had been living in her new space for just six weeks when I met her. She told me that she'd

Bonnie Conklin

With so many beautiful things— art, furnishings, rugs, and a cat— Bonnie Conklin's living room was not nearly as inviting as it could have been, nor did it show her prized possessions to best advantage.

Before ▲

always worked with decorators in the past and was now simply unable to visualize how to make her furnishings, artwork, and accessories fit into this new space as well as they had in the last. But she also loved her things and wanted to be able to use as many of them as possible.

The Diagnosis

Bonnie had placed her sofa across from the entrance on what happened to be one of the shorter walls of the living room, and perpendicular to the window wall. To the side of the sofa farthest from the windows was a tall decorative screen. At the end closest to the window was a drop-leaf end table with a few accessories and a Chinese ginger jar lamp, which provided the only reading light for the sofa. In the corner next to that was a tall plant. Because the eye was forced to move from the tall screen to the low sofa and then the taller plant, the items on that one wall were creating a roller-coaster effect. In front of the window, at right angles to the sofa but facing slightly away from it, were a club chair and ottoman, with a pharmacy lamp to the right of the chair. Although the sofa and chair constituted a conversation area, it would have been difficult for two people to converse without the one on the chair having to twist around to face the person on the sofa. The conversation area was anchored by a fairly large oriental rug and a round, glass-topped coffee table centered between the sofa and the chair.

In the corner beside the window Bonnie had angled a writing desk with a nice brass lamp. On the wall next to the desk, across from the sofa, was a very handsome built-in unit with open shelves above, on which she had both books and accessories, and closed

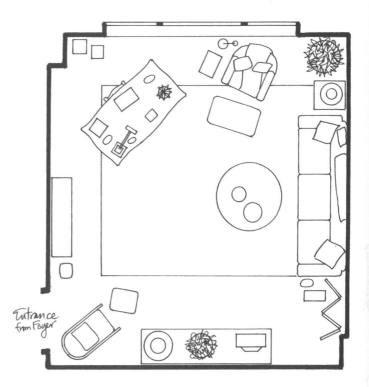

Entrance from Foyer

Before

storage below. And on the wall opposite the windows she had a long, low storage chest that held her television, VCR, and cable box as well as a tall candlestick lamp, a vase of flowers, and two or three additional accessories. (It was perhaps indicative of Bonnie's inability to decide how to use her things that she hadn't yet removed the price tag from the lamp shade.)

73

This wall of furniture, art, and accessories lacks an essential focal point that would hold it all together.

Above the chest she'd hung a panoramic black-and-white photo of the Brooklyn Bridge and next to that a large oil painting of a seated woman. Beneath the painting, to the right of the chest, was a rocking chair.

Bonnie had some lovely artwork and tasteful accessories, but neither had been arranged to create any real sense of balance or cohesiveness.

The Mistakes

- Uncomfortable conversation area
- Furniture of different heights
- Ignoring the focal point
- Lack of balance
- Lack of cohesion
- Improper use of artwork
- Ineffective use of accessories
- Inadequate lighting

The Remedy

The first thing we did was to move the sofa so that its back was to the windows not only to conceal the radiator and air-conditioning unit but also as the first step to create a more inviting and balanced arrangement. We then repositioned the main furniture in a more comfortable U-shaped conversation area by placing the chair and ottoman facing one another at either end of the sofa. The rug still anchored the space, and the coffee table in the middle was now accessible to all.

We then moved the end table so that it was between the club chair and the sofa, providing an additional resting place for a glass or a book, and positioned the pharmacy lamp behind it to serve as a reading light.

We left the plant in its original corner and surrounded it with a themed collection of rattan baskets that had previously been scattered around the floor.

We put the desk at an angle in the corner of the short wall where the sofa had been, facing the windows. Now,

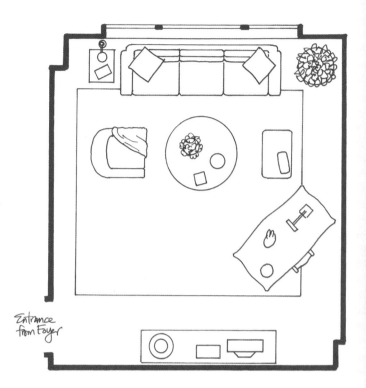

Entrance from Foyer

After

when Bonnie sits at her desk, she can look up and see all the greenery outside.

The oil painting that had been above the sofa actually continued to work well where it was, now behind the angled desk and the ottoman. And to give the arrangement greater presence, we paired it with the smaller

75

Shifting the main pieces of furniture
not only created a comfortable conversation area but also hid distracting
elements such as the air-conditioning
and heating units under the window.

After ▲

"I never would have thought of that!"

Hanging the two similar oil paintings next to one another: "I love the way those paintings look together. And now I can see them so easily when I'm sitting on the sofa," said Bonnie.

Putting the bronze sculpture on the corner of the writing desk: "That sculpture has always been one of my favorites," Bonnie commented. "It would never have occurred to me to put it on the desk because it's so tall, but it looks just great and I'm going to enjoy looking at it while I'm writing."

painting that had been on the small piece of wall next to the windows.

We replaced the long photograph on the wall above the chest with a second painting by the same artist that was already on that wall, which complemented the portrait of a woman. Now the seated ladies in the two paintings almost seem to be conversing with one another. In addition, we removed everything except for the TV and video equipment from the top of the chest and exchanged the tall candlestick lamp for the shorter Chinese ginger jar, which is in better proportion to the chest and also allows you to view the painting above it without any obstruction or distraction.

Then, we removed all the accessories from the writing desk, leaving only the lamp on one side and a largish bronze sculpture. The look was much cleaner, and the sculpture brought some height to that corner of the room.

Finally, we removed many of the accessories that had been scattered about as well as some of the decorative pillows, the patterned throw from the sofa, and the rocking chair, which was really too informal for the room. The decorative screen that had been creating too much of a roller-coaster effect was moved to Bonnie's bedroom. The Brooklyn Bridge photo and the rocking chair also moved into the bedroom, where they were actually more appropriate.

The furniture, which had previously been angled every which way, is now much more balanced and, therefore, has a more orderly and calming effect. And, with some of the extraneous accessories removed, the whole room feels more elegant and the pieces that remain are shown to much better advantage. In addition, the view outside remains unobstructed and can now be enjoyed from the chair and the ottoman as well as from the writing desk.

Long-Term Recommendations

To complete the conversation area and introduce much-needed pairs for greater balance, I suggested that Bonnie purchase a pair of small end tables in the same wood tone as that of the desk as well as a pair of table lamps with off-white linen or silk shades for either end of the sofa.

I also recommended that she replace the wooden blinds with semi-opaque linen-colored pleated shades that could be lowered from either the top or the bottom. Not only would they be lighter than the blinds, but they also could be lowered from the top to hide the air conditioner and still let in light as well as the view during the cooler months.

And because she'd mentioned that she didn't really love the long chest on the right wall, I suggested that, when she was ready, she replace it with a piece of similar size in French or transitional style.

For more flexibility, she could have tight-fitting slipcovers made for the upholstered furniture in off-white cotton/linen fabric so that they could be removed and cleaned, and she could put castors on the club chair and ottoman so that they could be moved as necessary to accommodate more guests.

Putting the plant in a navy or celadon porcelain pot and covering the topsoil with Spanish moss would give it a more finished look. And then, for greater drama, she could highlight it with an up light.

▲ After   Placing the two complementary
paintings in this unusual arrangement
not only is dramatic but also provides
the balance that this wall needed.

I also recommended that she have all the photos in the built-in unit framed in the same material and, finally, that she consider replacing her television with a flat-screen model to hang over the storage chest. If necessary, she could then move the two oil paintings to the bedroom.

THE CLIENT'S REACTION

I like my things—I even love my things," Bonnie said, "but I really didn't know how to make the space feel good, so I just threw up my hands.

"I can't believe the transformation. It's so peaceful and so soothing, and what's wonderful is that now I can really see some of the pieces that mean the most to me and enjoy them more.

"What I really like so much is that I now have a detailed plan to follow," she exclaimed. "I've really learned a lot about decorating from this meeting."

8

Room to Grow

MORE SPACE, MORE CHALLENGES

The Clients and the Complaint

John Duff and Brian Levy

"This place is much larger and more open than our previous apartment, which was very compact, and we're not sure how to set up the main room," John Duff said when I met him in what was then still the raw space of the building he and his partner would soon be occupying. "Although many people wouldn't think so, moving from a smaller to a larger home is as much of a challenge as downsizing. I know that some of what we have isn't going to work, and we'll have to buy some additional pieces, but we'd like to use as much as we can so long as it looks right."

A few weeks after the initial consultation, track lights and sconces are in place, and the room is getting its first real paint job.

John and Brian's previous apartment was compact but full of light from large windows.

The new space under construction: John and Brian were already looking for ways to use what they had to make this much larger space feel homey.

Before ▶

John is a tall, lanky, impeccably dressed publishing executive in his fifties with the quiet good manners of a Victorian gent. His partner, Brian, is an attractive, curly-haired fifty-year-old physician with a twinkle in his eye who doesn't hesitate to express his likes and dislikes. They seem to balance one another perfectly, and together they share a love of good food, theater, and travel to exotic locations.

Because John is so organized, he had photographs of their current apartment showing the pieces he and Brian intended to bring with them, which meant that, at our first meeting, we could discuss placement as well as the additional purchases they would have to make. Normally I have only one meeting per room with a client, but in this case I knew I would return to help John and Brian with the finishing touches.

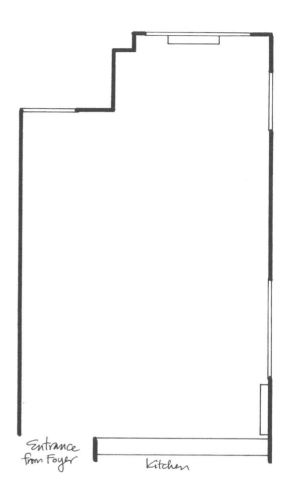

Before

The Diagnosis

There is a small foyer that opens to a large (21 by 33–foot) living room/ dining area with an open galley kitchen to the right that is separated from the rest of the space by a counter. There are double north-facing windows at the far end of the room as well as a single window. And on the right-hand, east-facing wall there are double and single windows.

Because of the northern and eastern exposures, I realized that the room would be relatively dark for much of the day, and the main room, while certainly spacious, was also somewhat unwieldy because it didn't define itself architecturally in any way, so that it would have to be structured by the layout of the furniture.

The Remedy

Starting with the basics, I suggested that they cover the windows with pleated linen Duette shades that could be opened from either the top or the bottom and paint the walls a light creamy color to brighten the room. I also recommended that they get white track lighting with tiny white halogen spots so that there would be nothing large suspended from the ceiling to break up the space. For the same reason, I told John they should leave the hardwood floors bare (and polyurethane them every couple of years) except for a 10 by 12–foot

Tibetan rug they already had to define and anchor the conversation area.

John and Brian shop in spurts and can go for months without buying a thing, but now they knew they would need to purchase a long, light-wood dining table to replace the smaller, square, marble-topped table but one that would still go with the modern chairs they already owned. The chairs, which were ready for a sprucing up, would be reupholstered in taupe ultra-suede for easy care. The table and chairs would be placed directly in front of the entrance on the left-hand wall, where they would be most easily accessible to the kitchen. Over the table they planned to hang a large oil painting of a Greek landscape by American artist Laura Hussey. Sconces from their old apartment would flank the painting to reinforce this focal point.

They also owned an old Canadian pine hutch for storing their serving pieces that would look lovely with two botanical prints hung above it at the far end of the long left wall, near the window.

To make the conversation area in the far corner more interesting and

inviting I recommended that they angle the whole arrangement slightly
toward the entrance on the opposite
side of the room. The beige-colored
L-shaped sofa they'd had in their last
home would go in front of the windows with a painted screen they had
purchased and a couple of leafy bamboo trees. Across from the sofa would
be two round-armed barrel chairs in a
coordinating taupe woven fabric that
were also from their former living
room and, to its left, two ottomans upholstered in the same taupe ultrasuede
as the dining chairs to form an almost-
square seating arrangement with a
glass and cherrywood coffee table in
the middle. In their previous home the
table had been configured as two
smallish triangles, but now there was
enough space for it to be fully opened
into a square.

For task lighting (beyond the more
general track lighting) I suggested a
pair of table lamps that could be placed
on end tables to flank the conversation
area. As it turned out, however, they
purchased one decorative table lamp
to stand on a nest of bamboo tables for
the right side of the seating area and a

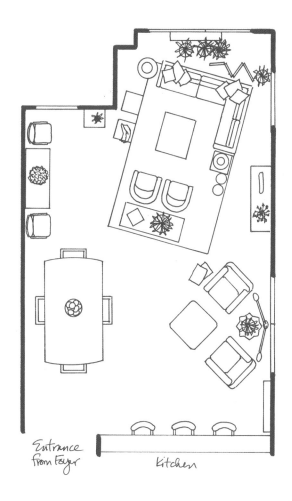

Entrance
from Foyer

Kitchen

After

hammered-metal standing lamp that
they placed next to the arm of the sofa
at the opposite end.

That still left a significant amount of
empty space. For the long right wall
between the east-facing windows, I
recommended they purchase a 5- or

85

6-foot sideboard that would provide good closed storage as well as a place to display accessories and anchor a piece of artwork. Then, for the same side of the room but closer to the kitchen, I suggested they create a reading niche with a matching pair of comfortable, oxblood leather armchairs and a single ottoman. They already had a round, Moroccan painted-wood table to place between the chairs, and they would purchase a double-headed, brushed-brass pharmacy floor lamp to stand behind it. Since reading is important to both John and Brian for their work, I felt it was important that they have this cozy spot as an alternative to the more formal living room area.

And, finally, I thought they should buy three stools to place on the living room side of the counter, where they could have a light meal and people could gather for drinks and hors d'oeuvres. That way, when they were entertaining, the hosts wouldn't be isolated in the kitchen during final meal preparation while their guests were seated in the conversation area at the other end of the room.

Twelve months after moving in, all the items on the Use What You Have® plan have been completed. But, as John and Brian discovered, a home is always a work in progress.

◄ After

87

After ▲

The most used area in the apartment—a comfortable place to read and chat.

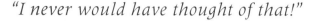

"I never would have thought of that!"

To create a reading niche with the two leather chairs in front of the east-facing window near the kitchen: "We both work long hours, and our home is our refuge," said John. "When we're there we spend as much time sitting in those two chairs reading or talking as we do in any other spot."

Angling the conversation area toward the entrance: "We knew we wanted the seating in the back section of the living room, but we didn't realize how much more welcoming it would be just by rotating the whole thing on an angle," Brian said.

The Ultimate Result

With all of the furniture, accessories, and artwork in place, it was clear that the solutions we'd envisioned in the empty space had been remarkably successful. Now it was just a matter of fine-tuning.

John and Brian purchased a low painted Chinese wooden chest that was so beautiful they decided to put it behind the two barrel chairs in the conversation area, where it immediately draws the eye and also serves as a distinct "line of demarcation" between the living room seating area and the rest of the space.

The finishing touches in that area were just to raise the lamp on the bamboo nesting tables with a couple of art books so that it would "read" as being the same height as the standing lamp, and to place a couple of Chinese figurines next to it to dress it up a bit.

The sideboard was perfect on the right-hand wall, and above it they'd hung a large abstract lacquered print. When I arrived, I took two small oil paintings of a café in Buenos Aires from the shorter section of wall closer to the kitchen and rehung them on either side of the print. The eye now has a place to rest on the shorter blank wall, and the print has been made to look more important. The pair of metal deer sculptures on top of the sideboard, which had also graced their previous living room, now perfectly complements the art. A bamboo serving tray on a stand that had been under the single north window to the left of the sofa was moved over to sit beneath two vertically hung contemporary Chinese lithographs. The tray itself was accessorized with a plant and a couple of family photos.

They'd had one wooden basket on the floor to the right of the sideboard and another to the left of the bamboo lamp table, so I put them both together next to the lamp table and removed a tray table that had been to the sideboard's left so that the main piece now stands out by itself. I also removed some of the throw pillows that had been on the sofa and brought in a chenille throw from the master bedroom to accent one of the ottomans and give the grouping a cozier feel.

Beyond that, a plate of fruit on the dining table, fresh flowers all around, and a few accessories like the turquoise-blue dish on the painted chest, picked up the colors in the rug and added splashes of brightness to the neutral walls and furnishings.

THE CLIENTS' REACTION

We pretty well agree about almost everything. Although I prefer fewer pieces of art on the walls than Brian does," admitted John. "But we're both extremely pleased with the result.

"We weren't sure how to fit what we already owned into our new place or what we should buy to maximize the space both practically and aesthetically. Now we're happy to see how well the various areas have been defined and how spacious it still looks."

"The space has been used really well," Brian said. "It still has an open feeling, but it's intimate, not vast. It's comfortable for the two of us, and it's also good for entertaining. When we have company we can move the ottomans around for more seating. Our new home really suits all our needs now."

9
Better Safe than Sorry

CHILDPROOFING WITH STYLE

The Client
and the Complaint

"I love all the things I have here, and for a while I thought it felt pretty good, but now I feel that I need to do something but I just don't know how to change it." Elaine Fernandez had worked with Use What You Have® fifteen or twenty years ago and said she'd learned a lot, but now she was doing something new and she needed more help. A widow in her sixties who is an administrative assistant for a major financial corporation, Elaine loves her work and finds it very gratifying. But she also loves her eighteen-

Elaine Fernandez

Elaine loves all of her things, but they were not giving her the pleasure that she'd hoped for. And now that she has got a lively grandson visiting often, the room is not as child-friendly as it could be.

month-old grandson, Jack, very much, and she wants her daughter and son-in-law, who live in Pennsylvania, to visit as often as possible.

She mentioned to me that, on a previous visit, her daughter had been concerned that some of the furniture as well as the many accessories displayed in her home could be dangerous for Elaine's naturally curious

toddler grandson. That was the impetus for her to call us, but the more I talked with her the more obvious it became that she was also seeking more comfort for herself. She did everything from watching television to listening to music to reading in her living room, so it was especially important to her that the room work well.

Before ▼

The Diagnosis

One of the main reasons for Elaine's discomfort was, no doubt, the fact that she had a very uncomfortable conversation area. There was a sofa on the right-hand long wall. The sofa was flanked by a Windsor chair to the right and, to the left, by a white silk-covered chair with wooden arms that was angled away from the sofa. In front of the window stood a round bamboo folding table and, angled in the window corner, a settee with a Victorian marble-topped pedestal table and a lamp behind it. At the other end of the room were a club chair and ottoman facing into the center of the room, but both this chair and the settee were far enough away to be at shouting distance from the sofa. In addition, the trunk that was serving as a coffee table was so close to the sofa that it would be uncomfortable for anyone to sit or walk in front of it. The area rug in front of the trunk did not anchor the space as it should have. Elaine read in the club chair, but from there she couldn't watch the television, which was in the wall unit.

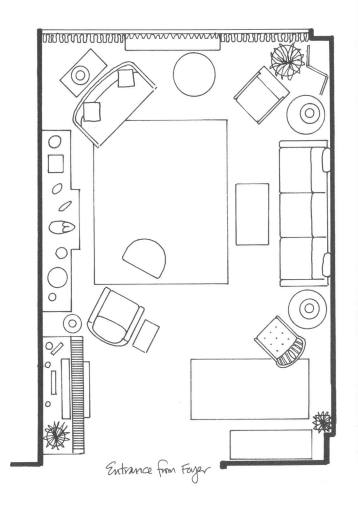

Entrance from Foyer

Before

The other furnishings in the room included an upright piano side by side with the large wall unit, a very pretty folding screen tucked into the corner, and a skirted table with a glass top that held a lamp with a flowered shade

93

and several accessories. The piano was creating much too much weight on the long wall near the wall unit, while the bamboo folding table, the screen, and the skirted table all presented hazards for the toddler. On the near short wall, opposite the windows, there was an antique pine chest as well as a small mahogany corner table with a large porcelain planter holding some greenery.

Finally, there were several large accessories high up on top of the wall unit, making it look even taller. Artwork was scattered on virtually every wall, and there were two smaller rugs in addition to the one in front of the sofa that chopped up the space. One of the smaller rugs, Elaine told me, "belonged" to her fourteen-year-old pug dog, Oscar.

Elaine's problem was an overabundance of riches, so to speak—too much furniture, too much bric-a-brac, and too many things hung on the walls at different heights, creating a roller-coaster effect and allowing the eye no place to rest.

The Mistakes

- Uncomfortable conversation area
- Poor furniture placement
- Awkward traffic pattern
- Ignoring the focal point
- Ineffective use of accessories
- Improper use of artwork

The Remedy

First we had to create a more comfortable and functional conversation area. To do that, we separated the club chair and ottoman, putting the chair at the near end and the ottoman at the window end of the sofa to create a U shape. The tile-topped table went into a corner in the foyer, where it would be less of a hazard for Jack. In addition, we moved the rug closer to the sofa with the trunk on top of it to help anchor the new arrangement.

After that, we removed the dangerous bamboo folding table from in front of the windows, and I suggested that Elaine keep it tucked away in a closet at least until her grandson was older. There were no window guards, but by centering the piano in front of the windows, we accomplished two more goals: taking a lot of weight off the long left wall and creating a focal point that would block the windows from the inquisitive toddler. We left the ficus tree in the corner next to it and created a display of family photos on top of the piano.

The settee was moved to the space next to the wall unit where the piano had been. Much smaller and more delicate than the piano, it doesn't add weight to that wall. With a standing lamp next to it, we created a cozy secondary conversation area.

The silk-covered armchair went into the far-left corner next to the piano. The Windsor chair was moved farther into the near-right corner by the pine chest. Both could now be easily pulled up as needed for additional seating.

And then there were the screen and skirted table to deal with. First, we removed all the artwork from the wall behind the sofa and stood the screen there instead. Fully open, the screen was more visible than it had been in the corner, and held in place by the sofa, it posed no threat to Elaine's

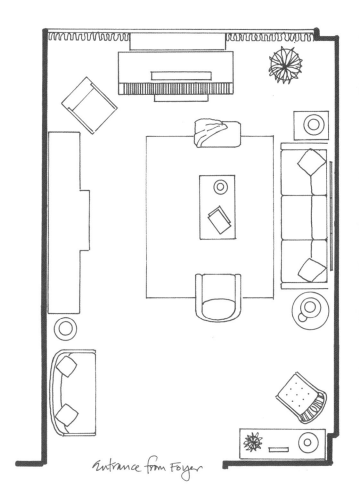

entrance from Foyer

After

grandchild. Then we played "musical tables": We removed the cloth (one less thing for the baby to pull on) from the round, skirted pedestal table and put the glass directly on the tabletop to protect it. Then, we moved the table itself to the right side of the sofa. The rectangular Victorian marble-topped pedestal table, which had been hidden behind the settee, replaced the skirted table on the left side of the sofa, and the smaller round table from the right of the sofa was moved across the room next to the settee. Placing two more or less simple lamps of similar scale with similar white shades on the end tables created the illusion of a pair.

We moved the small corner table and planter from near the entrance to the bedroom. Then we took all the art off the walls. Elaine didn't mind "losing" most of the prints. In the end, we hung two of her favorite pieces in very pretty gold-leaf frames, one on top of the other, between the sofa and the Windsor chair to create a sense of balance by mimicking the height and verticality of the screen. On top of the chest, we placed the blue lamp with the flowered shade that had been on the skirted table along with a pair of antique brass birds that Elaine had received as a gift from her mother, a silk flower arrangement, and a framed invitation to a surprise birthday party that had been held in her honor. Above it we hung two prints, one directly above the other, which will eventually be replaced by a painting of Elaine's late husband and a drawing of herself that is being reframed.

Finally, we removed the two smaller rugs as well as the flounced valance that had been hanging between the curtains and all the accessories from the top of the wall unit. We also repositioned the floral pillows so that they pointed upward at either end of the sofa instead of standing on top of its backrest, and we moved the large watercolor that had been above the piano to hang above the white chair between the wall unit and the window wall.

Not only is the room now much safer for Elaine's grandson, it is also

"I never would have thought of that!"

Putting the screen behind the sofa: "Before the screen was hidden behind everything. I love the screen behind the sofa," said Elaine. "Now I can see it, but it's not a hazard for my rambunctious grandson. It's an A+!"

▲ After   Almost all of the existing furnishings
and artwork were used to transform
this room into a more comfortable,
and safe, environment for everyone.

much more calming and comfortable for her.

Long-Term Recommendations

In addition to reframing the drawing of herself to match the frame of her husband's portrait, I suggested that she reframe the photos that we'd arranged on the piano that were not already in silver to give the display a more elegant and cohesive look.

I also suggested that she paint the walls as well as the curtain pole linen white and the ceiling white to make it look higher.

If she decided to replace the rug anchoring the conversation area, I recommended that she buy one that was slightly larger. In addition, she could use the tones of the small rugs from her hallway. And, since we'd removed the one that belonged to Oscar, I suggested that she buy him a monogrammed dog bed of his own to replace it.

Other than those few additional changes, I recommended that she have the end tables touched up in places where there had been some damage to the finish and purchase some Spanish moss for the base of the ficus tree and the silk flower arrangement on the pine chest.

THE CLIENT'S REACTION

Elaine was thrilled with what we'd accomplished and amazed that there was so little left for her to do. "I love it just the way it is," she said. "This is perfect! I don't have to do a thing." And she was certain that she would not have been able to do it on her own. "I don't think I would have had any of these ideas. It will definitely be better for my grandson, but it's also softer now and there are more pretty places where people can sit down and have a comfortable conversation. In fact, it looks like a magazine. What a difference!"

10

Life Goes On

NEW CAREER, NEW PETS, NEW LOOK

Jack Kupferman with Zim and Bobway

The Client
and the Complaint

"The situation here has become impossible! I love my things, I love my pups, I love my home, but nothing seems right. I just can't deal with the dog and decorating issues anymore."

Jack Kupferman is a lawyer in his midforties who had worked with another designer from Use What You Have® several years before. When he called again, his life was changing. He'd just become a "daddy" to two miniature pinscher puppies named Zim and Bobway; he was leaving the practice of law to start a magazine (called *Geri*) geared toward helping senior citizens and their families as well as a website for eldercare professionals; and in the years since he'd last worked with us, he'd acquired a lot more things. The pieces he had didn't seem to be working as well as they could, and he was particularly concerned that the puppies, which he loved dearly, were "messing everything up."

Gregarious, intense, and effusive, Jack is the kind of guy who, once he decides to do something, doesn't do it halfway. After his partner died, he was motivated to "get in shape" and started taking aerobics classes. In 2001, he won the National Aerobics Champion-

The loose coverings on the furniture and an assortment of bric-a-brac made this living area feel chaotic rather than comfy.

Before ▼

ship for men thirty-five and older. Now he'd decided to upgrade his living space and couldn't wait for us to get started.

The Diagnosis

Jack lives in a very small space composed of one main living/dining room, a sleeping alcove, a kitchen, and a bathroom.

At the far end of the room, in front of the windows, he had an overstuffed deco-style sofa with some plants behind it and a pharmacy lamp to its right. Coming straight out from the sofa lengthwise was a Chinese red rug with a colorful border, and at the opposite end of the rug, slightly to the left, was a club chair. He'd put a tray on top of the matching ottoman to use as a coffee table. He'd covered the seating with raspberry-colored throws to protect the upholstery from the dogs. The throws were not only loose and rather messy looking but also clashed with the rug.

The round oak pedestal dining table was placed at the near end of the

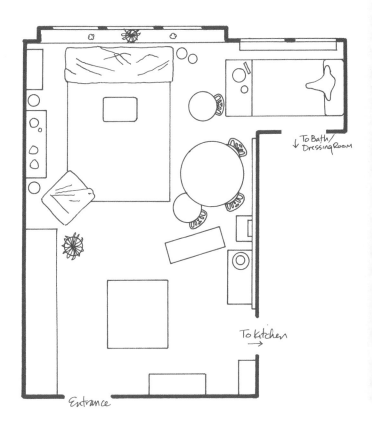

Before

right-hand wall. The four bentwood chairs that go with it were scattered around the room. Standing next to the table was a music stand with a light and, beyond that, a painted chest holding a glass lamp, the bust of a child, and a tiny tray. Above the dining table was a long display shelf that held a few matching prints. On the

▲
Before ►

above: Making a multipurpose space work well is challenging. This sleeping alcove off the main room needed fine-tuning to separate it visually from the rest of the space without closing it off entirely.

right: Things seem to have been scattered haphazardly around the room, taking away any sense of peacefulness as well as hiding the value of individual pieces.

same wall, a print in a black wood frame hung above the chest.

Beyond that were louvered doors to the kitchen and then, filling the rest of the wall, a bookcase holding files and a variety of odds and ends.

Against the entrance wall was a small bamboo pedestal with a wood top holding a display of photos, a vase, and books. A Kandinsky poster in a chrome frame hung above the pedestal table, underneath which sat a large black urn. To the left of the en-

trance was a row of three covered file boxes. Next to the file boxes was a tall armoire topped with an assortment of pottery, plants, and bric-a-brac, which housed a television. On either side of the armoire stood a pair of torchiere lamps.

In the corner to the left of the windows was Jack's Grandma Lucy's sewing machine—one of his prized possessions—which has been kept exactly as she left it, with all her needles, thimbles, and threads and even her

World War II ration card in the drawers. Jack told me that he'd been very close to his grandmother and that she had been the driving force in his life when he was a child. She'd had a newsstand on the corner of 25th Street and 8th Avenue in Manhattan, and he had an old, framed street sign from that corner as well as a photo of her at the newsstand and his grandparents' wedding photo, which were scattered throughout the room.

▶ The bedroom alcove at the far end of the living/dining room was separated from the living area by a long low dresser in a light wood that held a wrought-iron sculpture, a couple of framed prints, and a plant in a plastic pot. The bed was framed by a large wall unit, also finished in a light wood stain, with blue-painted insets and a round mirror in the center to mimic a headboard. The unit provided a substantial amount of closed storage and was actually a very clever use of space. A narrow shelf under the bedroom window also held a variety of accessories.

To back the dresser Jack had used a piece of tie-dyed fabric he said he loved and enjoyed seeing from his bed, but he also felt that it ought to be put in a place where it could be shown off to better advantage.

The Mistakes
- Improper use of artwork
- Ineffective use of accessories
- Lack of cohesion

The Remedy

One of the first things I did was to remove the loose throws from the upholstered furniture so that it looked less lumpy. While the mink-brown velvet sofa didn't match the burgundy chair, there were, fortunately, touches of both colors in the border of the rug. I then turned the rug on an angle to make it appear more elegant and graceful. I also removed the two smaller rugs, which had been chopping up the floor space and not really serving any useful purpose.

103

His primary mistakes were those that I've found to be the most common: putting lots of bits and pieces all over the floor and the surfaces so that the eye has no place to rest and the space feels chaotic.

We started by gathering up some of the stuff: We placed the large black pot from the entrance and another smaller one I found together behind the club chair. Then we removed all the objects from the top of the armoire and replaced them with one flat wicker basket to make the height of the armoire "read" the same as the height of the window. We also removed all the plants from behind the sofa and moved three of them in similar pots to the bureau separating the living room from the sleeping area. We grouped the remaining plants together in the corner by the sewing machine. On top of the sewing machine we arranged several wooden objects that had been in various places throughout the room. When I'd completed the vignette, Jack actually gasped and made me stop what I was doing so that he could take a moment

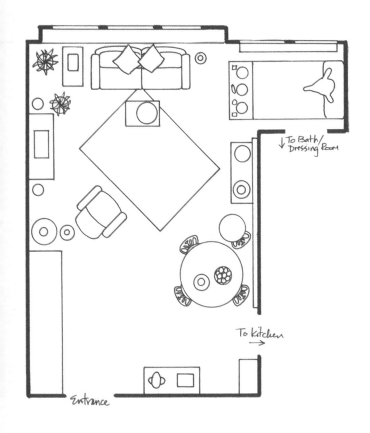

To Bath/
Dressing Room

To kitchen

Entrance

After

In the end, however, the configuration of all the main pieces of furniture remained almost exactly as it had been. My principal effort was to help Jack clear the clutter that had grown up around him over the years so that his room would be more peaceful and cohesive and the things he loved would be shown to best advantage.

▲ After   Starting with a better arrangement—
and getting rid of unnecessary clutter—makes a dramatic difference in
the look of this space.

Then we did the same thing with a few tiny stone objects—a horse, a seal, and a piece of slate—by grouping them on the bureau with the plants and a couple of prints in similar frames. The easiest way to turn chaos into calm and to create an elegant appearance is to group like objects together.

Then it was on to the dining area, where we created a vignette on the display shelf of all his memories of his grandmother, which included the framed street sign and his grandparents' wedding photo, which we clipped to the frame of the picture of her at her newsstand. The grouping also included a photo of Jack holding his nephew as a newborn baby, a framed Herb Ritz photo that had been standing on the floor next to the armoire, a photo of Jack in his aerobics outfit, and a few other objects that were the most meaningful to him.

We moved the bamboo pedestal table under the display shelf and transferred the music stand to the far left wall next to the sewing machine, where it could be used as a display piece. We put the painted cabinet beside the entrance and hung a Mexican

This room retains lots of character, reflecting the taste and interests of its owner, but well-displayed memorabilia and cleaned-up surfaces make it feel much more serene.

After ▲

to admire how well these disparate accessories now worked together. "I can't believe this," he blurted out. "Just because those things are all made of wood they look *amazing* together! Oh my God, I can't believe how happy I am!"

106

painting in a dark wood frame over it. On top of the cabinet we put the lovely bust of the child and an attractive wooden box Jack could use as a receptacle for his keys and a place to put his bills and other important mail. To complete the "family corner" near the dining table, we placed another photo of his nephew as a little boy on the bamboo pedestal along with a glass vase and the glass lamp that had been on the painted cabinet.

In the sleeping alcove, we spread the tie-dyed piece of fabric that had been tacked to the back of the bureau on top of the white bedspread so that Jack would be able to enjoy it all the more. The blue in the fabric picked up the blue of the wall unit, and it looked very attractive on the solid spread. There were two gold-colored square European pillows on the bed. On top of these I lay Jack's childhood stuffed animal—a large blue manatee—and hung his aerobics medals from the manatee's tail. We removed the miscellaneous items from the shelf under the window and replaced them with a group of brightly painted, carved wooden pieces he'd collected on trips to Mexico.

Because Jack had so many things that were precious to him and he wanted to be able to see and enjoy them, all the "stuff" in his home had simply overwhelmed him. Gathering these disparate accessories, collectibles, and meaningful memories into small vignettes for display restored order to the chaos and enabled him to enjoy both the things he owned and the tranquillity of his living space. Although he had perceived the puppies as his problem, the two "min pins" were really acting as his wake-up call— the latest acquisitions, so to speak, that

"I never would have thought of that!"

Creating a display on the shelf above the dining table of memories of his grandmother: "Now everything on this shelf is representative of what's most important to me in my life. You have no idea what it means to me to be able to enjoy them all together like this."

A few simple changes make the
sleeping alcove much more compatible
with the rest of the space. In particular, the new arrangement on top of the
bureau provides much needed order
and balance.

After ▲

let him know things around the house had gotten out of control.

Long-Term Recommendations

To accommodate his furry babies, I suggested that Jack have fitted slipcovers in cotton or linen made for all the upholstered furniture in the same golden color that was in the rug and the tie-dyed fabric on the bed so that they would look neat but could easily be removed and cleaned as necessary.

Since most of the floor space was now bare wood, which not only made the room look more open but also was better for the puppies, I recommended that he have it sanded and polyurethaned for easier cleaning and upkeep. He could also then take up the red wool rug for cleaning in the spring and replace it with the lighter, gold-colored one for the warmer months.

To improve the reading light and to add balance to the room, I suggested that Jack get a second, matching pharmacy lamp for the other end of the

sofa, or, if he couldn't find one, purchase a new pair.

To add those final but all-important elegant touches, I recommended that he have a travertine marble top (which would also be more durable) made for the painted chest in the entrance and that he purchase matching brass knobs for the cabinets and closet doors as well as a brass cover for the front door lock.

For the sleeping alcove, I suggested he dye the bedspread blue, which would tie into the painted unit as well as the tie-dyed fabric (and show less dirt than the white), and that he permanently sew the fabric to the spread. Then, to coordinate the color scheme with the fabric even more, he could purchase new, gold-colored sheets and a tangerine neck roll or sham to add to the pillows already on the bed.

To complete the sleeping alcove, he could mount two tiny halogen spotlights on the unit for reading, and, since we'd removed the fabric, he could back the dresser with a light maple or oak veneer to finish it off.

He could also purchase two small

matching monogrammed dog beds to put on the floor under the windows so that the pooches would have their own special space near his bed.

And to tie the whole color scheme together, I recommended that he have slipcovers made in a dusty aqua for two of the throw pillows on the sofa and purchase an aqua tassel for the lock on the armoire. The dusty aqua would pick up the color in the border of the living room rug as well as the blue of the bed unit and would become an accent color throughout the entire space.

THE CLIENT'S REACTION

Jack was not only amazed by the transformation we'd accomplished simply by cleaning up and rearranging his possessions, he was, in fact, truly moved by the use we'd made of his beloved objects. If ever a person's home reflected who he was at heart, it was this man's.

He had also confessed to me that he hadn't been entertaining much because of the way things looked, but he loved to cook and now wanted to have friends in to share his newfound pleasure in his living space.

"I can't get over this," he marveled as he walked around, admiring his home. "I was feeling really down and upset, but now I feel fabulous! You didn't just change my home; you've actually changed my life today."

11

Country Goes City

MOVING FROM A HOUSE TO AN APARTMENT

Maria Lamattina

The Client
and the Complaint

"How am I going to get through this without making expensive mistakes? It really is bothering me. I'm very concerned about all the things I could do wrong with this space." When I arrived for her consultation Maria Lamattina had been living in her new home for just a week. She'd painted the living room only two days before, and most of the furniture was still in the middle of the floor. I could see why she was throwing up her hands.

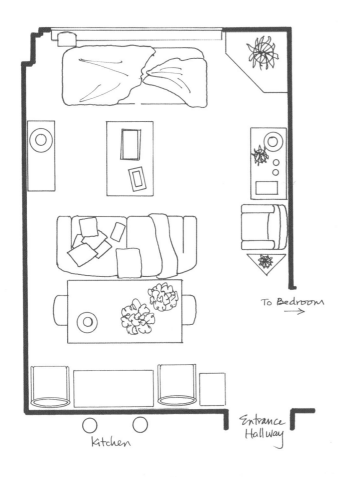

To Bedroom
→

Entrance
Hallway

Kitchen

Before

could tell right away that once she decides to do something, she gets it done. But her surroundings are important to her, and so, when it came to her new home, she wanted not simply to get it done, but to get it done *right*—the first time.

The Diagnosis

Maria had a lot of pieces in the romantic country cottage style she loves, but many of them were oversized, and it was clear from the start that she wouldn't be able to use *everything* she had. I did assure her, however, that I'd help her to keep as much as possible. She loves the overstuffed, slipcovered look, which meant that she had a sofa with wide, oversized arms and dining chairs slipcovered in white fabric with long ties at the back.

Since nothing had been arranged yet, we got to work putting her furnishings, art, and accessories in the places where they would look and feel best.

A vivacious woman in her mid-fifties with long dark hair and a big bright smile, Maria was trying to fit what she'd had in her previous, much larger home into a much smaller apartment. She's an extremely dynamic and articulate woman, and I

Before ▲

The Remedy

We began by placing the sofa on the long wall opposite the entrance, flanked by two smallish wooden end tables. Maria also had a pair of tall, slim lamps, which we put on the end tables behind a pair of matching silk flower arrangements. The floral arrangements fooled the eye into seeing the lamps as not so tall and provided a more proportionate horizontal plane.

Trying to fit a lot of furniture into a new, smaller space made this place look more like a jumble sale than the elegant room that it might have been.

113

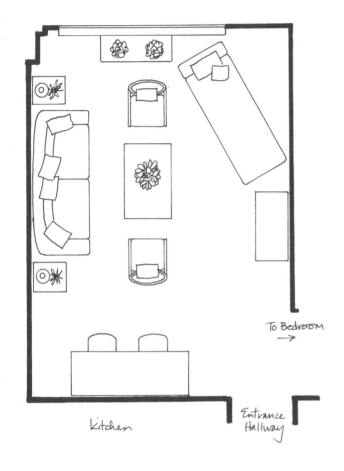

To Bedroom →

Kitchen

Entrance Hallway

After

To complete the U-shaped conversation area, I found a pair of pretty wooden armchairs with upholstered seats. Then we centered her black-painted coffee table in front of the sofa, where it was also accessible to anyone seated in the chairs. The table itself, although very attractive, was

really too big for the space, but it went well with the rest of the furnishings and would do nicely until Maria decided whether or not to replace it.

Now she had a pair of tables, a pair of lamps, a pair of flower arrangements, and a pair of chairs, all of which gave the area great balance.

We'd originally considered hanging a mirror over the sofa, but when Maria showed me a beloved oil painting of a young girl in a beautiful gold-leaf frame, we decided to use that instead. On either side of it we hung two smaller paintings in similar gold-leaf frames, which, together with the larger one, formed a charming focal point for the room.

Maria also had a lovely chenille-covered chaise lounge, which we angled to the right of the windows opposite the sofa. Again, it was a bit oversized, but it looked very pretty in that location. A few needlepoint pillows on the sofa, a couple on the chaise, and one on each of the wooden armchairs finished accessorizing the seating area.

The next order of business was to move the very pretty painted wooden

▲ After   The effective use of pairs and judicious editing of furniture and accessories—sometimes it is not possible
to use *everything*—really gives this
room classic charm and refinement.

"I never would have thought of that!"

Putting the flower arrangements in front of the lamps to give them a better scale: "I love my flower arrangements, and it's amazing that those two on the end tables actually make the lamps look so good!"

chest that she'd temporarily placed on the long wall near the windows. We swung it around so that it was centered under the windows, where it now blocks the central air unit from view. Maria, who loves painted furniture and that chest in particular, was very happy to be giving it such a prominent place in the room. On top of the chest, we created a display with a porcelain clock surrounded by a second pair of flower arrangements, a pair of candlesticks, and a grouping of family photographs.

The kitchen is separated from the living/dining room area by an open counter. I pushed the dining table up against the wall under the counter on the living room side and positioned the two dining chairs on the outside, facing toward the kitchen. The table can be pulled out when needed. Slipcovered folding chairs will provide extra seating. For her everyday use, we put a metal lamp on the table along with a green plant, so that it looks attractive and she can use the lamp to read or work at the table if she wants.

The painted armoire would be moved into the bedroom, and a large bookcase that was too big for the space would be put into storage. A triangular corner table that didn't fit in the living room could be used as a bedside table or stored.

Long-Term Recommendations

When Maria had mentioned that she was considering putting in crown molding, I suggested that it should be very thin, so as not to make the ceilings appear any lower than they are, and that she paint the molding the same semigloss color as the rest of the trim.

I recommended that she have a carpenter build in low bookcases under the window that extend all the way to the walls on either side of the painted wooden chest. To give the window treatment a softer look, I also recommended that she replace her vertical blinds with shades that could be opened from either the top or the bottom to provide both light and privacy.

Maria had a nice old low chest of drawers that I suggested she paint and put on the wall opposite the sofa with a flat-screen television hung above it. She could then put the club chair she had to the right of it. Her small bookcase next to the chair, with a candelabra lamp on top, would provide a surface next to the chair and light for reading.

Although there were several lamps in the room, the light was really not adequate. I suggested that she put in a track with five or six tiny halogen spots going from the entranceway to the dining area. And, for task lighting, she could increase the wattage of the bulb in the lamp on the dining table to 75 watts and put three-way bulbs with 150-watt capacity in the lamps on either side of the sofa.

If she decided to purchase a rug for the conversation area, I recommended that it be a neutral color and no larger than 6 by 9 feet. In addition, if she replaced her existing coffee table with a smaller one in an oval or drum shape or even with a trunk, it would be in better proportion to the size of the room.

Since she is so fond of painted furniture, I suggested that she paint the dining table and put on a glass top that would look very pretty and also protect the surface.

As for the partition above the counter separating the living area from the kitchen, I recommended that she put five matching clay pots and saucers filled with ivy or even wheat grass lined up across the top to fill in the open space and complement the country garden motif she'd already established.

THE CLIENT'S REACTION

When we were done, Maria was thrilled with the order we'd brought to her new home and delighted that we'd managed to use so many of the things she loved. "It's amazing to me," she exclaimed, "to see how out of all this chaos you were able to create balance and elegance. I really feel like this has been a collaboration: You asked my opinion and really cared what I thought. I love that we have been able to use almost everything."

12

Living Well in Limbo

MAKING THE BEST OF A TEMPORARY RENTAL

Marguerite Loucas, with her
daughter, Isabelle

The Clients
and the Complaint

"I feel as if I just crammed in all the furniture from the previous apartment, plunked it down, and because there are so many demands on my time, there it stayed."

Marguerite Loucas, a restauranteur, has flashing brown eyes, a dry sense of humor, and a devilish grin. She may be petite, but as soon as I met her I got the feeling that she was a real firecracker who did things in a big way. And my first impression was confirmed when I saw hanging on the wall in the

With drop-dead views and lots of wonderful pieces, this room has tremendous potential, but with a new baby and demanding jobs, the Loucases couldn't focus on what was wrong and how to fix it.

hallway a framed copy of the article from the Sunday "Styles" section of the *New York Times* describing the couple's courtship and lavish wedding.

When I met with the Loucases, they had been living in their current apartment for a year with their eleven-month-old daughter, Isabelle. Marguerite complained that she hadn't had the time to make their

present living space as attractive as she wanted it to be.

Since the Loucases had been looking for a house to buy and were in a rental, they didn't want to spend a lot of money on permanent fixtures that couldn't be moved. They do, however, like to entertain and to have their family visit often, and Marguerite wasn't happy with the way things looked.

Before ▼

"I'm frustrated because there's baby formula all over everything and the place is disorganized," she lamented. "It's a mess. A light switch just went on, and I realized I'm living in a mess."

Her discomfort went beyond the living room to include the dining area and bedroom, and she asked for help with all three.

The Diagnosis
THE LIVING ROOM

Marguerite Loucas likes and owns beautiful things, among them some lovely Lalique glass, very good artwork, and a nice collection of sterling-silver–framed photos in the living room. The room itself is spacious. The focal point is a continuous wall of curving windows that provide a dramatic, panoramic city view. But those windows also posed a unique decorating challenge. Because the curve of the walls goes all the way from the far left-hand corner of the living room to the near right-hand corner at the end of the dining room, the only straight wall is the one behind the sofa.

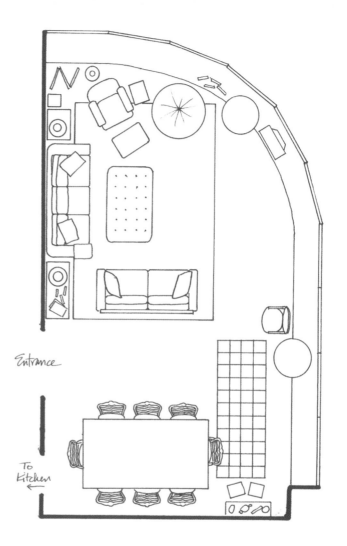

Entrance

To Kitchen

Before

While it was clear Marguerite was exaggerating when she said the furniture had just been "plunked down," the room did lack cohesion, and she

121

had made a number of the most common decorating mistakes.

The conversation area was comprised of a sofa set against the long wall with a love seat at right angles to it, its back to the entrance. A club chair and ottoman along with an additional round ottoman sat at the window end. Not only was the sofa and love seat combination extremely uncomfortable for conversation—arranged in the dreaded L shape—but the bulk of the loveseat put too much weight at the near end of the room, throwing it off balance and creating a poor traffic pattern by obstructing the entrance: all-in-all, very bad feng shui.

Adding even more weight to the near end of the room was a large chest to the left of the sofa, which was not properly balanced by the screen and small table with cabriole legs that were to the right.

And then there was the issue of too many ottomans. In addition to the ottoman that matched the club chair and the round poof, there was a rectangular tufted ottoman serving as a coffee table. Definitely ottoman overkill.

A large Aubusson rug that ran parallel to the long wall anchored the conversation area. The rug was lovely, but there was just too much furniture crowded on top of it. And, in addition, it was fighting the unusual shape of the room, trying to create right angles where there were really curves.

The artwork was hung at different heights, creating a roller-coaster effect over the sofa; there were too many pieces of Lalique bunched together on top of the chest; and the photos were displayed on the windowsill, where it was almost impossible to see and enjoy them. A lovely large carved-wood–framed mirror was hiding behind the screen near the windows, where it served no real purpose except to detract from the artwork and compete with the view for attention.

The Living Room Mistakes

- Improper furniture placement
- Uncomfortable conversation area
- Poor traffic pattern
- Room off balance
- Lack of cohesion
- Improper use of artwork
- Ineffective use of accessories

The Remedy
THE LIVING ROOM

The first thing we did in the living room was to reposition the rug so that it was on an angle, starting in the corner near the windows and moving away from the wall toward the entrance. By freeing the rug from the wall we allowed it to flow with the shape of the room rather than fight it. And, with more of the wood floor visible, the room immediately seemed more open and graceful.

Next, we moved the love seat from the near to the far end of the room with its back to the windows and replaced the heavy club chair and ottoman as well as the round poof with the two French chairs from the bedroom, which we positioned at the near end of the room with a Chinese pedestal chest displaying a gold-leaf wooden box—both of which had been hidden behind a screen—set between them.

Again moving the weight from the near to the far end of the room, we switched the chest and the leggy table on either side of the sofa. Under the

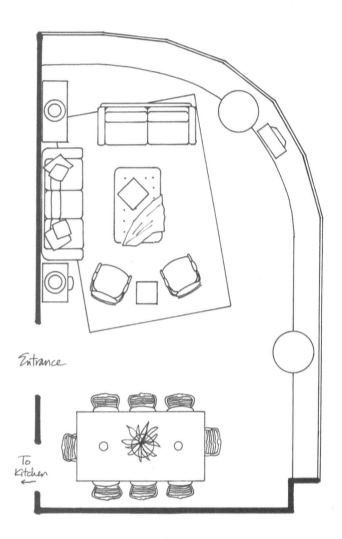

After

table we placed a beautiful hinged box that had been on top of the chest and a small footstool behind it to hold a stack of art books. By filling in the

Harmonious and well balanced, the new arrangement shows off the fine pieces of furniture and art and is immediately more welcoming.

After ▲

"I never would have thought of that!"

Angling the rug so that it made the conversation area more welcoming and didn't fight the curve of the room.

open space under the table we were able to balance the weight of the chest at the other end of the sofa and still create an airier look.

Suddenly, one felt invited into the room. The conversation area was now easily accessible rather than blocked by the back of the loveseat, and the view through the open chairs was un-obstructed. Good feng shui!

The two green-shaded table lamps remained at either end of the sofa but were better balanced by setting the one on the short table on top of two art books so that it would be at the same height as the one on the chest.

We left the tufted ottoman to serve as a coffee table because it was a good size and didn't have any sharp corners that might hurt the baby. We did, however, set a sterling-silver tray on top to display a few of the Lalique pieces that had been on the chest. (I

suggested that Marguerite bring the sterling tray out when she had guests and simply leave a chenille throw or a more utilitarian, baby-safe tray with a couple of art books on the ottoman for day-to-day use.) The round poof was removed (Marguerite said she would give it to one of her siblings), as was the screen that had been at the window end of the room. The club chair and ottoman, along with the standing lamp, were moved into the bedroom.

Finally, we tackled the rest of the artwork and accessories. We re-arranged the paintings over the sofa, lowering the large center piece by a couple of inches, adding a fourth smaller painting that had been hang-ing in the hallway for better balance, and moving all the smaller side pieces in closer to the large one. All of the throw pillows—the two that had been on the sofa all along and the two that had been on the loveseat—were arranged on the sofa with their corners pointing up toward the artwork. Now, instead of creating an uncomfortable roller-coaster effect, the artwork served as a secondary focal point for the room. The superfluous mirror was moved to the dining room, where it would be displayed to much better advantage.

The silver-framed photos were moved from the windowsill to the top of the chest, where they created a lovely collection. The windowsill itself was left bare, and the window was left uncovered to take full advantage of the spectacular view.

Long-Term Recommendations

The only thing left to be done in the living room after less than two hours spent rearranging what Marguerite already had was to increase the wattage in the two table lamps from 60 watts to 150 watts for more effective task lighting.

The Diagnosis
THE DINING ROOM

The main problem in the dining area was both immediately obvious and easily remedied. Marguerite had effectively turned a substantial portion of the room into a play area for Isabelle, so that the table and chairs were stuck against a wall playing second fiddle to a large, colorful children's rug as well as a play kitchen and other toys. Once that mistake was remedied, it took half an hour to create an elegant, properly accessorized space.

The Mistakes
- Improper furniture placement
- Lack or ineffective use of accessories
- Bad lighting
- Lack of cohesion

The Remedy

The simple and immediate solution to the obvious problem in the dining room was to free it from the clutter

Before ▲   A casually elegant dining table and chairs seem abandoned in this space and are made even less attractive by the incongruous play area set up in the corner.

of Isabelle's toys by moving them into her own room. I suggested to Marguerite that if she wanted to keep a few things in the dining room for the baby to play with, she could buy a hinged wooden chest in which to store them out of sight when they weren't in use. With the toys gone, it was a simple matter to move the table and chairs to their rightful place in the center of the room.

On the wall that faces the living

127

After ▲

With the baby play space moved to a bedroom and the simple addition of a dramatic mirror and tabletop display, the entire complexion of the dining area has been changed.

128

room, we hung the wood-framed mirror horizontally. This opened up the space by reflecting a view of the entire length of the living room all the way to the windows.

The new, more elegant look was completed in less than thirty minutes by bringing in a few of the larger pieces of Lalique to serve as a centerpiece on the table along with a vase of flowers and a pair of candlesticks.

Long-Term Recommendations

I suggested that Marguerite replace the ceiling fixture with a white track holding five halogen lights that could be adjusted to highlight the centerpiece and other areas of the room.

I recommended that she buy a three-foot-tall porcelain or hammered metal urn to fill with tall branches and set it on the windowsill for dramatic effect. And, as a place to display more of her lovely accessories and keep them out of the baby's reach, I suggested that she purchase four matching shelves in the same wood finish as the mirror and hang two on either side of it. To complete the look and give the space more drama, she could paint the wall in a warm coral color to tie in with the coral in the living room rug, which was visible from the dining room.

None of these suggestions would be difficult or expensive to carry out, and they would provide the balance and cohesion Marguerite was missing in her home.

"I never would have thought of that!"

Painting the dining room walls the same coral color as that of the living room rug.

129

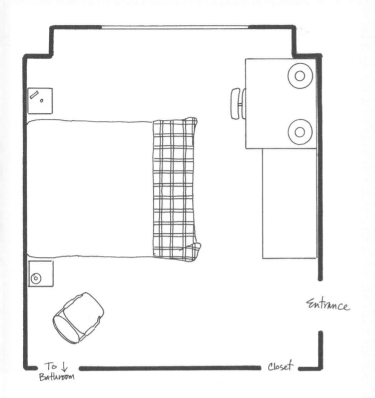

The Diagnosis
THE BEDROOM

The Loucases appeared not to have decorated the bedroom at all. There was no headboard on the bed, and the wall behind it was completely empty, with only a couple of small paintings hung vertically on a beam next to the window. Two tiny French tables served as bedside tables, but only one of them held a lamp, so that one person had absolutely no reading light at all.

Across from the bed, an armoire held the television, and next to that, nearer the window, was a desk on

Before

This bedroom feels so temporary and neglected— waiting for even a little attention.

Before ▼

130

which stood two brass-trimmed table lamps that were so tall they actually overpowered the desk itself.

There was a French armchair angled next to the bedside table with the lamp, but it served no real purpose (it certainly wouldn't have been an inviting or comfortable place to curl up and read) while its mate served as an equally uncomfortable desk chair.

Although it would take additional work to complete, there were several things we could do immediately that day to make the room function better and achieve a more polished look.

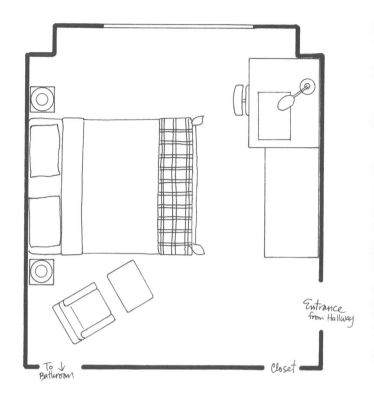

To ↓
Bathroom

Entrance
from Hallway

Closet

After

The Mistakes

- Inadequate lighting
- Ineffective use of artwork
- Lack of cohesion

The Remedy

The club chair and ottoman brought in from the living room immediately created an inviting and comfortable place to read on the left side of the bed. And two tall lamps, taken from the desk and placed on the bedside tables, provided much better reading light. Meanwhile, the standing lamp brought in from the living room would serve as a work light for the desk. To finish the wall above the bed, we hung the three oil paintings in carved-wood frames

"I never would have thought of that!"

Using the tall lamps from the desk on the bedside tables.

with gold-leaf accents that had been scattered on the other walls and grouped them to balance the height of the lamps. And, finally, we remade the bed itself to serve as a more attractive and decorative centerpiece for the room. Without our doing anything else, what had been a rather nondescript space looked much more pulled together and attractive quickly.

The Long-Term Recommendations

To complete the effect of the room, I recommended that Marguerite paint the wall behind the bed a camel color and that she slipcover the club chair and ottoman in a solid toast shade, both of which would coordinate with the Burberry throw on the bed. She would also buy new, coordinated bedding, including a duvet, sheets, king-size pillows, neck rolls, and a bed skirt.

To replace the French chair that had been moved to the living room, I recommended that she buy an armless black leather desk chair on wheels for the desk.

And finally, while moving the table lamps had already improved the bedside lighting, I recommended that they also be fitted with three-way switches for greater flexibility.

After ▶

All it took was a pair of lamps, a chair and ottoman, a simple arrangement of paintings, and a remade bed to transform this room in minutes.

THE CLIENT'S REACTION

Marguerite was delighted at how quickly we'd been able to banish the "mess" she felt she'd been living with and create a more serene, finished, and elegant environment. "I can't get over how much more open all the rooms feel. Now, instead of focusing on the baby formula on my chairs, I can just enjoy how nice and organized everything looks." In less than four hours we'd pulled together three rooms without requiring her to spend very much money on things she wouldn't be able to take with her when the family moved to a new home. She said that while the apartment had previously been yet another chore demanding her attention and contributing to her nagging sense of frustration, it was finally a place reflective of her taste where she could rest, relax, and enjoy being with her family and friends.

13

Staying On While Moving Up

PUTTING AN END TO THE DORMITORY LOOK

The Clients and the Complaint

"Our kitchen may be the smallest one in the city, and we don't really spend a lot of time in our bedroom, so our combined living and dining room really gets a lot of use. We love having the big window overlooking the garden, and we're happy with our sofa and the colors we've picked for the throw pillows. The problem is that we just don't feel comfortable with the way the space is set up and we haven't any idea how to make it better. Plus, I'm starting a new job in a couple of weeks,

Monique and Michael didn't want to spend a fortune to improve the look of their rental.

and I'd love to get this place together while I still have some free time."

Monique and Michael are writers in their thirties and both work for large international corporations. They are lucky enough to live in a lovely turn-of-the-century brownstone building, in a space that has a working fireplace and a garden. It is, however, a rental, and although they plan to stay there at least two or three more years, they wanted to improve the space without investing in too many structural changes that they'd have to leave behind if and when they moved.

The Diagnosis

The main room is multifunctional, serving as living room and dining area. To the immediate left of the entrance are a closet and an uninterrupted wall. An audio/video unit is tucked into the

In spite of some interesting architectural details, the living/dining area still had a transient feeling to it.

Before ▼

▼ Before ▶

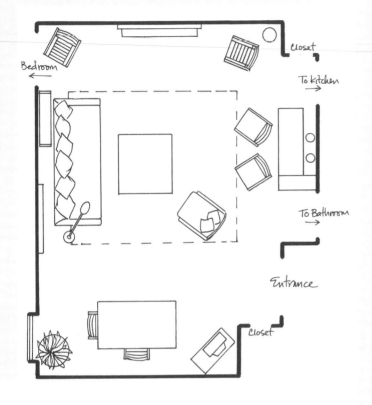

Before

placed across from and at an angle to the sofa made up the conversation area. A light beige rug that was clearly intended to define and anchor the seating area actually gave the impression of cutting the room in half because it ran across the center of the floor and was shorter than the wall to which it was parallel.

On the right-hand wall of exposed brick is a very lovely stone fireplace with carved reliefs. It should have been the focal point of the room but was being largely ignored and further obscured by too many accessories. Two dining chairs and an umbrella stand appear to have been abandoned against the wall on either side of the fireplace.

A small, cluttered breakfast bar and two stools stood between the doorway to a tiny kitchen and the entrance.

One of the most obvious problems was that the furniture was poorly placed so that the room's various functions remained undefined, in addition to which the main traffic pattern of the room cut directly through the conversation area. The artwork, all of which was framed in black, was hung indi-

corner beside the closet, angled into the room, and the dining table and two chairs stand between the unit and the window wall. Other dining chairs are scattered around the room. On the wall opposite the entrance, the sofa was placed between a large window overlooking the garden and the passage to the bedroom and bath. The sofa, a bentwood coffee table in front, and a midcentury woven wood chair

vidually on every wall, and accessories were scattered around the room.

The Mistakes

- Poor furniture placement
- Poor traffic pattern
- Lack of cohesion
- Ineffective use of accessories
- Improper use of artwork

The Remedy

As is often the case, we began by rearranging the furniture. We moved the sofa to the center of the wall to the left of the entrance, opposite the fireplace. The woven wood chair was positioned with its back to the window and perpendicular to the sofa. We moved one of the dining chairs opposite the woven chair to create a U-shaped conversation area, which was anchored by the rug, with the coffee table in the center. The standing lamp that had been in the window corner behind a plant was moved to the left of the sofa along with a wide, flat basket that had been next to the fireplace to serve as

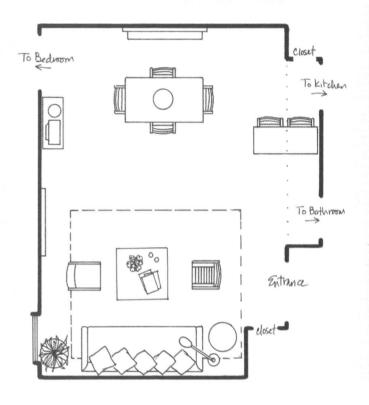

After

a magazine holder. The plant now stands alone, under the window to the right of the sofa. Moving the main seating not only took advantage of the room's true focal point, the fireplace, but also created an open passage from the entrance through the room to the bedroom without interfering with the conversation area.

To take advantage of the black-framed artwork that had been scat-

139

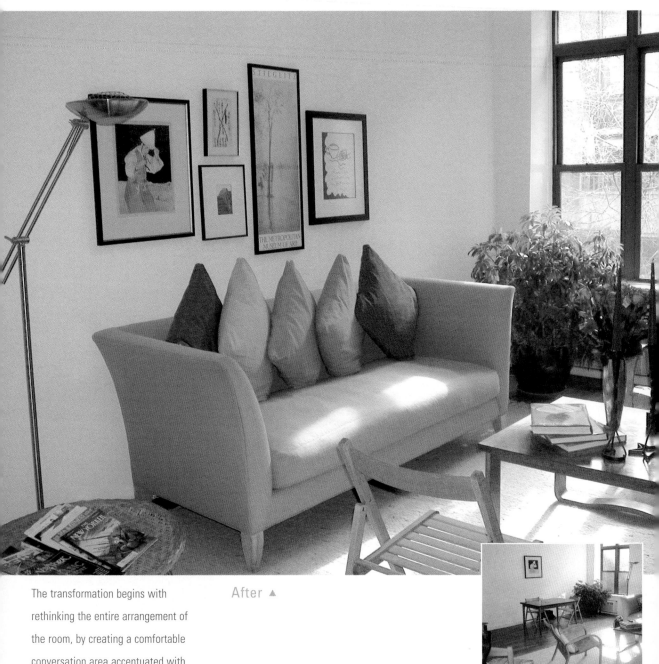

After ▲

The transformation begins with
rethinking the entire arrangement of
the room, by creating a comfortable
conversation area accentuated with
an effective grouping of art above
the sofa.

tered here and there, we gathered it all in a single grouping behind the sofa. The throw pillows on the sofa were re-arranged so that they point upward, drawing the eye to the artwork.

The dining table and all four of its chairs were moved to stand in front of the fireplace, where they are also more convenient to the kitchen.

The wheeled audio/video unit now occupies the wall where the sofa had been, with a single horizontal piece of art over it to balance the height of the window.

We turned the counter near the kitchen so that it is now perpendicular rather than parallel to the wall and put the two stools on the kitchen side so that the area could be used either as an eating space or as a work surface for food preparation. The clock that had been on the fireplace mantel now hangs over the counter.

▲ After

"Extending" the tiny kitchen into the main area was essential, but the rearrangement of the counter and a little tidying up made the space less distracting and infinitely more functional.

"I never would have thought of that!"

Turning the counter and enclosing the sides to conceal the garbage pail and improve the aesthetics of the work area: "This extension of the kitchen had always been an eyesore," said Monique. "But we really needed the counter space and couldn't figure out how to do this without a big investment."

The unusual placement of the dining table in front of the fireplace serves many purposes, yet the fireplace still remains the focal point of the room—as it was meant to.

After ▲

Once the clock was gone from the mantel, the painting, which had been hung much too high over the fireplace, could stand directly on the mantel. The candlesticks were moved to the coffee table and were replaced by additional pieces of colored glass, which had been scattered around the room, to create a small collection with the red bowl that was already there.

The only two items actually removed from the room were one small piece of art and the umbrella stand.

Long-Term Recommendations

Although we had moved one of the dining chairs to form a U-shaped conversation area, I suggested that Monique replace it with another woven chair to match the one she already had. Or, because she and Michael both are writers and love to read, they might replace both chairs with a pair of comfy club chairs or even recliners (I couldn't believe I was saying this, but there *are* sleek and attractive models available now!) in a height and fabric that would be compatible with the sofa.

I also suggested that if she and Michael planned to entertain more often, they might consider purchasing a slightly larger dining table and chairs with upholstered seats to replace their folding chairs. Or else they might add cushions and slipcover the folding chairs to give them a more stylish look.

To improve the task lighting and create a sense of balance, I recommended that they purchase a pair of end tables with closed storage space and a pair of table lamps with plain linen shades or two steel pharmacy lamps for either end of the sofa. One standing lamp could then be moved across to the fireplace side of the room to light the dining table.

In addition, I thought they ought to extend the existing track lighting to better highlight the work counter and entrance, brightening the end of the apartment that is farthest from the window.

While Monique and Michael were reluctant to spend too much money on built-in structures, I did suggest a

couple of relatively inexpensive ways to create much-needed additional storage as well as to improve the appearance of the room. First of all, they could create significant additional closet space by extending the closet next to the kitchen all the way to the fireplace. Exchanging the sliding doors for bifold doors would also enable them to view everything inside all at once. As I explained, the area was effectively unused space that had been taken up only by the now-banished piece of art and umbrella stand.

Then, if they were planning to stay more than just a couple of years, I thought they might consider building a large "loft" cabinet running over the top of the entrance door, all the way across the recessed area above the counter to the wall on the right, outside the kitchen. This would create copious, closed, long-term storage without reducing the floor space. Recessed down lights could then be installed in the base of the new overhead cabinet to highlight the counter.

To improve the aesthetics if they planned on living there several years, I suggested that they build a storage

143

unit running across the entire back wall, from under the window to the bedroom hall. Not only would this hide the air conditioner and radiator but also it would provide additional storage and a place to put their audio/video equipment and the flat-screen television they intended to purchase. A bifold door in front of the air conditioner could be kept closed in winter and opened only when the air conditioner was being used. Once the new television was in place, they could move the piece of art over the audio/video unit to the bedroom hallway. And if it was built in sections made to look like one piece, most, if not all, of it could move with them to their next home.

A final, relatively simple and inexpensive job for the carpenter would be to enclose the two exposed sides of the counter with pieces of wood stained to match the rest of the unit so that they'd be able to hide a garbage pail or a wine rack underneath and still have sufficient room to sit with their knees under the open side.

A white Silhouette shade installed inside the window frame would probably not be movable, but it would be a soft and unobtrusive way to provide them with privacy for the duration of their rental.

THE CLIENT'S REACTION

When we were finished, Monique stood by the front door with a big smile on her face. As she surveyed her reorganized living space, she said, "Everything feels calm and open now. The sofa has more natural light for reading, the counter area by the kitchen looks more inviting and comfortable, and even the table and chairs look great by the fireplace. I love the way the mantel looks with the colored glass paired with the poster, but my favorite is the grouping of art over the sofa. The whole arrangement is more sophisticated and pulled together."

14

Playful Elegance

SEEKING FORMALITY IN A CHILD-FRIENDLY SPACE

Sharon Mosse

The Client and the Complaint

"I'd love my home to have a very formal, elegant look, but at the same time I want my family to feel unrestricted and comfortable," said Sharon Mosse, a high-powered businesswoman who has held senior-level marketing positions in a number of major corporations, as she showed me into her living room. As so often happens, the inspiration to make a change had come at a turning point in her life, when she established her own marketing business and started working from home. She

and her husband, Fred Miller, a music producer, share the space with their son, Ben, an articulate and engaging little boy who was "seven going on eight" when we worked together.

"I'm glad we all use the living room to spend time together as a family and play games," she went on, "but every time I'm in here it bothers me that it doesn't look the way I want it to. Ideally, I'd like it to be beautiful for me, but also functional so that I don't have to worry when Ben brings his friends in to play. And I really hate the

▲ Before ▼

Fine furnishings and classical architectural details made this living room ripe for a positive change.

146

fact that it always seems so dark. We have a northern exposure, and I know we really need more light."

When Sharon began working from home, and consequently spending more time there, she became more aware of the fact that her environment was not truly reflecting her stage of life or that of her family. I was called in to help her "polish up" the living room and dining room to better mirror her own elegant style and make her feel happier to be spending so much more time at home.

The Diagnosis
THE LIVING ROOM

With its fireplace and grand piano, the large living room is gracious and well appointed. All the basics were, in fact, there, but they weren't being used or shown off to the best advantage.

The living room, which is also used as a family room, was formally furnished in traditional style but with a rather incongruous casual wood and glass coffee table that was doing double duty as a storage space for Ben's

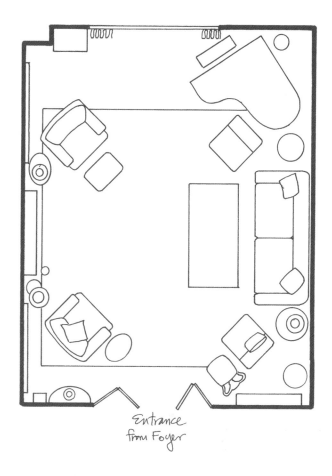

Entrance from Foyer

Before

toys and a large game not very well hidden, peeking out from behind the sofa.

Beyond that, however, the furniture itself was awkwardly placed. The sofa, which was on the long wall facing the fireplace, was flanked by two small similar-sized end tables, one of which held a ginger-jar lamp. And next to the tables, matching slipper chairs were set at angles facing toward the fireplace. Behind the chair to the right of the sofa stood a small bookcase, above which hung one of only two pieces of art in the room. (The other piece, a small very beautiful painting, was hung on a narrow wall next to the window, fighting for attention with the view.) A wooden chair, which seemed to have escaped from the dining room, sat in front of the bookcase next to the slipper chair, and another occasional table was tucked into the corner beside the bookcase.

To the right of the sofa, a grand piano occupied most of the window corner.

Opposite the sofa, a handsome fireplace, which was the main focal point of the room, was not having the kind of impact that it deserved. Two club chairs, one with an ottoman, sat on either side of the fireplace, facing toward the sofa, but neither was close enough to make for a comfortable conversation area. A small table with a lamp, along with an incongruous CD rack, sat behind the club chair to the right of

the fireplace. A floor lamp stood to the left of the fireplace.

Built-in bookcases occupied the wall space on either side of the fireplace, but neither was well appointed; a jumble of albums, framed photos, antique toys, and other odds and ends were displayed somewhat haphazardly.

The Living Room Mistakes

- Improper furniture placement
- Uncomfortable conversation area
- Ignoring the focal point
- Improper use of artwork
- Ineffective use of accessories
- Inadequate lighting

The Remedy

The first thing we did was to determine that most of Ben's toys and games could very well be kept in Ben's room, which had more than adequate space for storing them. Once they were removed from the coffee table, it no longer looked so out of place.

To create a more comfortable conversation area and better balance in the arrangement of furniture, we moved the club chairs closer to the sofa, forming a more intimate U shape, and replaced them with the less cumbersome slipper chairs, which we set as close to one another as possible flanking the fireplace. The coffee table remained in place but now is used to display a few attractive accessories rather than to hold a hodgepodge of games.

To provide better balance and better light, we moved a table that had been floating behind the club chair to the left of the sofa and moved the one that had been there to the right. They now held a matching pair of ginger jar table lamps. The two smallest tables flank the slipper chairs, where they give anyone seated a place to set a cup or glass. The standing lamp has been moved behind the chair to the right of the fireplace to provide better reading light on that side of the room.

Next we tackled the artwork and accessories. The wall above the sofa was crying out for something large that would anchor the conversation area. As an immediate solution, we moved in a large horizontal landscape from

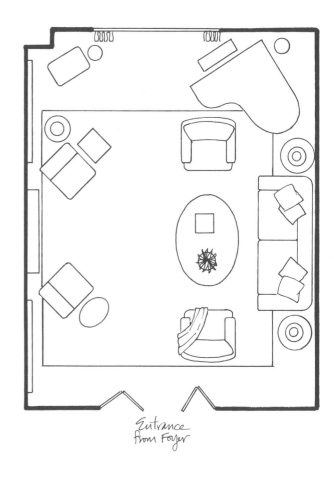

Entrance from Foyer

After

the dining room, even though it was not the ideal size.

The photo albums with matching bindings and all the framed family photos were placed in the bookcase to the left of the fireplace. I suggested that Sharon rebind the nonmatching books and reframe the photos that didn't match the others. In the bookcase closer to the window we arranged all the art books and created a display of Fred's antique toys. The CDs were stored in the enclosed shelves below the books and toys.

To balance the height of the tall built-in bookcases and create a more arresting effect for the fireplace, we removed the mirror that had been hanging horizontally above it and stood it vertically, directly on the mantel, along with a beautiful piece of art glass that was one of the many items previously hidden on the small wooden bookcase. In front of the mirror we placed a pair of porcelain birds with matching candlesticks set to either side. (Sharon said that she would purchase some additional accent pieces to complete the effect.) The eye is now drawn to a more dramatic vertical display.

The two small paintings were moved to other rooms. The small bookcase that had been to the right of the door went into the master bedroom. The walls on either side of the entry are now left bare to create a resting place for the eye.

Long-Term Recommendations

To complete the new, more elegant look of the room, I suggested that Sharon replace the coffee table with something more in keeping with the other furnishings. We also discussed the possibility of purchasing a larger piece of artwork whose size would

"I never would have thought of that!"

Collecting all the silver-framed family photos in one bookcase and creating a cohesive display of Fred Miller's antique toys in the other: "The bookcases are really a handsome feature in the room," said Sharon. "Now they are shown to their best advantage, and we get to display our collection and photos effectively."

▲ After   Within a couple of hours, the true
elegance of the living room that had
eluded Sharon and Fred was revealed.

After ►

A very few new purchases—the coffee table that is more in keeping with the style of the other furniture, and sconces to create a dramatic arrangement with the painting above the sofa—brought out the full potential of this elegant living room.

This beautiful fireplace is no true focal point of the

better balance the length of the wall above the sofa or, alternatively, a pair of gold-leaf pedestals or a similar pair of objects to hang on either side of the existing painting to fill the space.

She said that she would purchase some additional accessories and would look into the cost of recessed lighting to create better general illumination for the living room as a whole.

153

The Diagnosis
THE DINING ROOM

Sharon knew that the dining room wasn't living up to its potential; she just couldn't figure out how to fix it. "I like our dining room furniture," she said, "but the space feels like a pass-through to the kitchen when it should be a gracious place to sit and eat. Fred and I both love to have dinner parties, but I just can't figure out what this room needs to pull it together."

Like the living room, the dining room opened off the entrance foyer through dramatic double doors. The oval mahogany pedestal dining table was placed on a large patterned rug. With all its leaves in place, the table took up an enormous amount of space

even though, on a daily basis, the family had no need for such a large table. All the dining chairs, except the one that had escaped to the living room, were pushed against the walls.

A marble-topped server stood on the long right wall, and over it hung a vertical mahogany-framed Victorian-style mirror flanked by a pair of sconces and a pair of small botanical prints.

The large window at the far end of the room was set off with curtains and

Fully extended, this handsome table overwhelmed all the fine elements in the dining room.

▼ Before ▶

drapery, but the windowsill was cluttered with a variety of mismatched accessories that detracted from the elegance of the window treatment.

And, finally, the chandelier over the table was fitted with bare bulbs that created a harsh rather than flattering light.

The Dining Room Mistakes

- Improper furniture placement
- Ineffective use of accessories
- Improper use of artwork
- Improper lighting

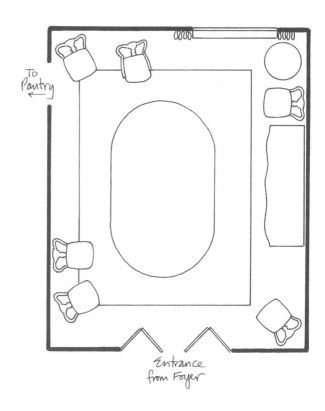

To Pantry

Entrance from Foyer

The Remedy

The first thing we did in the dining room was to remove one leaf from the table so that it no longer took up so much space on a day-to-day basis when it wasn't really required for family meals. We moved the lovely handpainted basin from the windowsill, where it stood with its matching pitcher, to the middle of the table and filled it with fruit. In addition, in a moment of inspired "set decoration," we placed a tea set on a silver tray at the end of the table closest to the door to make a welcoming gesture. We then arranged all the armless dining chairs around the table (retrieving the one escapee from the living room) and stood the two armchairs against the wall on either side of the server.

To create a more dramatic and elegant appearance for the server, we exchanged the two small botanical prints with two larger ones that had been in

Before

155

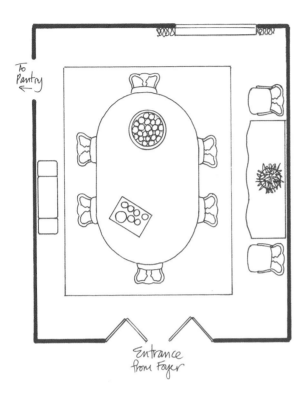

To Pantry ←

Entrance from Foyer

After

ror. Several silver dining room accessories that had been hidden away in a cupboard completed the display.

On the long left-hand wall, which needed to be kept clear as a traffic pattern to the kitchen, I hung the oil painting in the carved gold-leaf frame that had been ineffectively displayed on the window wall in the living room and flanked it with two prints that were in similar mahogany frames with touches of gold leaf. Below this grouping we set a narrow, upholstered bench that had been in the entrance foyer. The overall effect was to give the wall a finished look without blocking the way to the kitchen.

The lighting over the table was quickly made more flattering and restful by putting small shades on the bare bulbs in the chandelier.

Finally, we cleared all the clutter from the windowsill, leaving only the antique clock, which is now centered and showcased.

the bedroom. The scale of the larger prints was better suited to the space between the sconces and the mirror and the smaller ones were actually a better size for the bedroom. We filled the pitcher from the windowsill with flowers and stood it in front of the mir-

"I never would have thought of that!"

Switching the smaller botanical prints from the dining room with the larger ones from the bedroom: "This little detail really made a big difference," said Sharon. "And it really showed us how to use what we have!"

▲ After A few simple changes, including the removal of one leaf from the table, really bring this dining room together while showing off the exquisite individual pieces.

With virtually no expense at all, the room immediately looked more cohesive, more restful, and more elegant.

Long-Term Recommendations

Although Sharon and her family were delighted by what we'd been able to do so quickly, I did suggest that she consider installing recessed halogen lighting in the four corners of the room that would be controlled by a dimmer separate from that of the chandelier.

I also recommended that she re-upholster the dining chairs in the same fabric as the draperies so that the patterns wouldn't be fighting with one another and that she replace the sheer curtains with a semi-opaque linen-colored Duette shade that she could drop down from the top for privacy while still allowing light into the room.

The other purchases I recommended were a glass-and-brass drinks trolley that could be placed on either the window wall or the left wall and used for entertaining as well as a pair of hurricane lamps and a pair of pillar-style candles to complete the new display on the server.

THE CLIENT'S REACTION

Sharon was thrilled to see how quickly and easily her home could be made to look the way she had believed it could and should. While she was certainly considering all the additional touches I had recommended, she was astonished to see how polished these rooms looked already, even without any new furniture or accessories. "I'd hoped they would look more elegant," Sharon confessed, "but I never dreamed they could be transformed this quickly and effortlessly, especially without compromising their functionality. Now Ben will be able to play in the living room, and, at the same time, Fred and I will be able to enjoy the way it looks."

15

An Eye for Detail

COMPLETING AN ART COLLECTOR'S HOME

The Client
and the Complaint

"I know this may sound strange, but my space feels hostile to me. It's so bad that I almost never sit in my living room."

When she called me, Susan Ollila, a lovely willowy and elegant brunette who is Director of Fixed Income Investments for the Ford Foundation and a very serious art collector, had been living in her apartment on Manhattan's Upper East Side for about four years. It had been completely renovated at substantial cost, and, be-

Susan Ollila is a longtime collector of
American twentieth-century painting.

Before ▲

An elegant space that needs just a little fine-tuning.

cause Susan is so sensitive to subtleties of color, she'd called upon Donald Kaufman, the premiere colorist in the country and author, with Taffy Dahl, of the book *Color: Natural Palettes for Painted Rooms*, to select the interior paint colors.

She had begun to work with an interior designer, but when that relationship didn't work out, she'd left things as is for about a year. When she called me, Susan said that she wanted me to tell her why her environment felt so uncomfortable.

160

The Diagnosis
THE LIVING ROOM

One of the pleasures of doing my work is that I'm often able to learn while I help to educate my clients. Working with Susan Ollila was an interesting and educational experience for me because of the degree of sophistication and sensitivity she brought to every detail of her surroundings. It was interesting for me to find that even someone of such clearly refined taste and discernment was not able to determine exactly what it was about her living space that was making her unhappy and uncomfortable. As with any kind of "therapy" it may take a professional with a fresh and unbiased perspective to diagnose and help solve the problems.

The first thing that Susan wanted to talk about was the sofa. She wasn't happy with it and thought that the fault lay with the pale yellow color, which she believed fought with the sand and gold in her beautiful Tibetan rug. While I agreed with her assessment, it soon became clear that Susan's problem went beyond color to

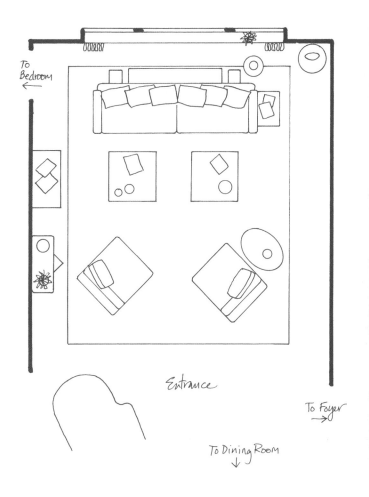

Before

the style of the sofa and also to her lack of comfort with the entire conversation area. The sofa itself was very attractive but much too deep for Susan to sit on comfortably. It would have been perfect for someone six-three or taller, but even at about five-nine she

161

would never be able to sit back on it without feeling awkward. She'd been aware of the problem and had already had an extra pad put into the back and added throw pillows to bring it forward, but it still wasn't working.

To add to her discomfort, the two chairs across from the sofa that completed the conversation area were too far away. Between the sofa and the chairs, two square Edward Wormley tables that had once belonged to a former editor of *House Beautiful* magazine were serving as cocktail tables. The tables themselves were exquisite, as was everything in Susan's home. The top of each one was set with one larger and two smaller tiles—the first Tiffany tiles ever produced—grouped together to form a square. The problem, however, was that the tables, while close enough to the sofa, were inaccessible to anyone sitting in the chairs. A small table next to the chair on the right could be used to put a drink on, but the person sitting in the chair on the left had nowhere at all to put anything. The chairs were also set at an angle that obstructed the traffic pat-

tern along the left side of the room, where the entrance to Susan's bedroom is situated.

Another piece that was disturbing her was a small leggy table on the left-hand wall under which she had placed a basket filled with pillows. She said she wasn't sure why it made her uncomfortable, but she just wasn't happy with the arrangement.

Oddly, perhaps, for such a serious art collector and someone so sensitive to color, Susan's lighting was also inadequate. While there was good general illumination, there was just one standing lamp behind one corner of the sofa, which was the only place anyone could read comfortably.

None of these were glaring mistakes, and they might have gone unnoticed by anyone less sophisticated and sensitive to her environment than she. It was interesting, however, that even Susan had not been able to put her finger on exactly what it was that had been bothering her.

The same was true of her artwork and accessories. They were individually lovely, and all of them were important and of the best quality, but things weren't working as well as they could or should have been. The accessories on the coffee tables, for example, were too small, and those on the windowsill were both lost and detracting from, rather than enhancing, the "living artwork"—the peripheral view of Central Park.

One of the most important pieces in the room was an Edward Wormley fluted wood pedestal that sat in the far right-hand corner next to the window. Designed to open up to a bar, it held one of her three Inuit sculptures (the other two were on the windowsill). Both the pedestal and the sculpture are beautiful objects, but it was almost impossible to absorb their importance because there was so much art in the room.

Her collection of early-twentieth-century paintings is one of the most important I have seen in a private home. She told me that the first piece she'd bought, a Doris Lee painting acquired while she was still in college, now hangs in her dressing room. In the living room there were, among others, a Fairfield Porter, an Allen Tucker, a James Caroll Beckwith, and—one of her favorites—a very colorful Jane Peterson painting of zinnias. In all, there were six paintings on the right-hand wall and one large one on the left wall, each so important and so beautiful that the total effect was overwhelming.

The paintings, she said, were like old friends, and they brought her, as she put it, "great joy and fun," so she was reluctant to remove even one or two of them because she wanted to be able to look at them every day. My challenge would be to bring her more peace while still allowing her to enjoy the plethora of artwork.

The Mistakes

- Improper furniture placement
- Uncomfortable conversation area
- Poor traffic pattern
- Inadequate lighting
- Improper display of art
- Ineffective use of accessories

A beautiful gallery of art is better
showcased when other elements of
the room work in harmony.

After ▲

164

The Remedy

The first thing we did was to move the chairs closer to the sofa and straighten them so that they faced it directly. We then moved the small table between the two chairs so that both people occupying the chairs would be able to use it. With these minimal changes, we created a more comfortable conversation area and also improved the traffic pattern on the left side of the room.

In the bedroom, I found a second standing lamp that matched the one behind the sofa. By placing them at either end of the sofa, not only did we improve the task lighting, but we also created a second pair that mimicked the pair of chairs, thus adding balance to the room.

Next, we addressed the problem of the small table on the left-hand wall that had been making Susan uncomfortable. We removed the basket of pillows from the floor underneath and replaced it with an antique wooden horse that had been next to a piano that sat in an open area between the

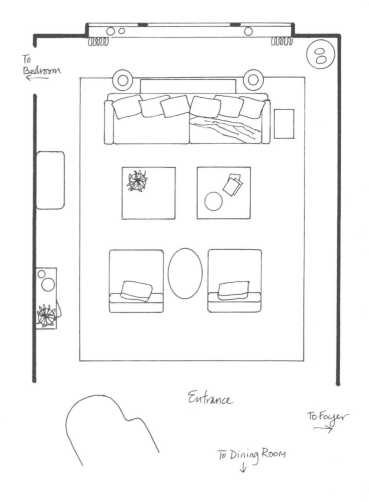

After

living and dining rooms, angling it so that you could see the horse's face as you entered the room.

Finally, we rearranged some of the accessories, replacing the small plant on one of the coffee tables with a larger one that had been on the windowsill and making a single stack out of several books that had been scattered in various locations. We brought over a couple of additional objects that had been in other places and filled a white porcelain bowl, which had been on one of the tables, with shell nuts. The result was that the scale of objects was a bit larger, and Susan, with her discerning eye, noticed the difference immediately.

None of these changes was extensive or revolutionary, and they might not have made so much of an impact on anyone else, but to Susan they were extremely important. She seemed delighted with each and every one of them and began to smile more and more. It was a pleasure for me to see how excited she became as we worked together.

at right: Subtle changes make a world of difference to the discerning eye, which Susan Ollila certainly has.

Long-Term Recommendations

Not just the color but also the depth of the sofa remained a problem for

After ▶

166

"I never would have thought of that!"

Raising the Wormley bar on a pedestal to give it more prominence.
Placing the antique horse under the table in the living room, where it would be seen better and more appreciated.

"God is in the details."

After ▲ —Mies van der Rohe

Susan, and she determined that the only way she would ever truly be comfortable in her living room was to replace it. She'd already begun to consider a few different models and showed me the photos she'd collected. I pointed out to her that a couple of them had uncomfortable arms, and I told her to be sure she sat down on each one before making any decision. One of them had a small pillow that would rest at the base of the spine, and I recommended that she remove it before testing the sofa for comfort because the pillow might be concealing the fact that it was too deep and would, therefore, present the same problem as the one she already had.

For color, I suggested a solid plum. The living room walls were a very pale celadon green, and I thought that the plum would be a beautiful complement for them as well as for the sand

and gold in the rug. Susan, with her exquisitely sophisticated color sense, had already considered a burgundy, but I thought the plum I had in mind would have even greater depth. As it happened, there was a Blanche Lazzell painting in the room that had a touch of the exact color I'd visualized. When I pointed it out to her, she knew immediately that it was the right choice. "That's exactly what I want," she exclaimed. "That's perfect. I love that color."

The last substantial change I recommended was that Susan have a pedestal made in rubbed gold leaf or ebony stain to put under the Edward Wormley pedestal bar in the corner. This would raise it up so that the Inuit sculpture displayed on top would be more visible and important. If she wanted, she could also have another small pedestal made in marble or painted wood to put under the sculpture itself, which would make the piece even more prominent.

My remaining suggestions were small but significant for Susan. Among them, I recommended that she have a couple of throw pillows made for the chairs in the conversation area to pick up the plum of the new sofa as well as the celadon of the walls.

There was an ottoman against the left-hand wall near the table, and I suggested that she put it on small brass castors so that it could be pulled into the conversation area if necessary when she had company. And I recommended that she buy a porcelain pot

THE CLIENT'S REACTION

This is astonishing to me! The room makes me feel relaxed now, and everything in it seems to relate to everything else. I can't wait to have you come back to do the other rooms."

Susan was so pleased with the small but, for her, immensely significant changes we'd made and with my other suggestions that she asked me to come back and work with her on the library, dining room, and master bedroom.

in plum, celery, or crackle beige for the plant on the floor near the bench to replace the basket it was in.

Although she remained reluctant to remove any of the paintings, she did agree that she might move one or two of those that were less important or meaningful to her to other rooms.

The Diagnosis
THE DINING ROOM

The room is beautifully proportioned and the furniture elegant, but it lacks a cohesive feeling.

While the rest of Susan's apartment needed only modest changes, the din-

Before ▼

ing room provided some significant challenges as well as at least one fascinating discovery.

Susan had told me that she liked to spread out and work at the dining table and that the one thing she specifically did *not* want was a traditional formal dining room, so I wasn't surprised to see that the room was very different in both furnishing and feeling from most of the dining rooms I see in my work.

In the open space to the right of the entrance, there was a small leather club chair next to a small table with a reading lamp, and to the left, a neo-classical wooden armchair, another of which occupied a spot near the window at the far end of the room.

Past the table and chair on the right was a bookcase filled with art books, leather-bound first editions, and some contemporary fiction as well as a variety of accessories. To the right of the bookcase hung *Leenane*, a large and important painting depicting Kilarney Bay by Paul Henry. To the left of the bookcase were four more oil paintings in gold-leaf frames. Across the room there was a large Doris Lee painting in

lavenders and mauves that complemented the colors in the cushions on
the wooden armchairs and the dining
chairs.

The nineteenth-century French oval
dining table and four metal bentwood-
style chairs were at the far end of the
room, turned perpendicular rather
than parallel to the long wall.

Because of the disparate chairs and
tables scattered about, the room
lacked cohesion, particularly with the
dining table at the far end and so
much empty space in the middle. In
addition, the bookcase seemed redun-

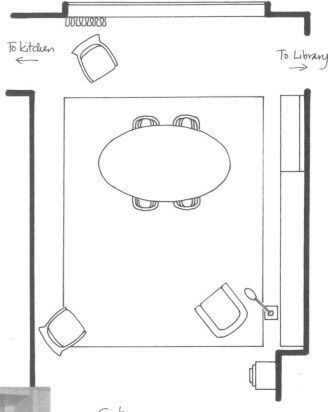

To kitchen ←

To Library →

Entrance

To Living Room ↓

Before

A bookcase can make a significant statement for any room, but
the scattering of books, objects,
and glassware does not create
a dramatic look, nor does it show
off the individual pieces well.

◄ Before

A simple and unusual arrangement of furniture quickly changed this room, making it more graceful as well as functional.

After ▲

172

dant, given the fact that there was also an entire wall of books in the library. And the accessories, some of which were quite important pieces, were lost among the books. Finally, there was no light at all over the table, which is where Susan often worked.

The Mistakes

- Poor furniture placement
- Lack of cohesion
- Awkward traffic pattern
- Improper lighting
- Ineffective use of accessories

The Remedy

The first change we made was to position the dining table so that it was angled with its left end closest to the entrance and its right end pointed toward the window—more or less in the seven o'clock/two o'clock position.

Next, we placed the two wooden armchairs in front of the window, facing into the room and angled toward

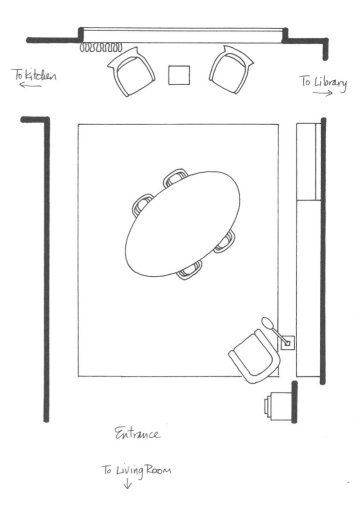

After

one another. Then we centered two metal and glass nesting tables that were not being used in the living room between the chairs so that the group-

173

The various elements are now effectively integrated, with the important and interesting pieces appropriately highlighted.

After ▲

"I never would have thought of that!"

Moving all the contemporary fiction to the library and displaying only first editions, art, and leather-bound antique books in the dining room, arranged to more dramatic effect.

ing could be used either for conversation or for reading.

To differentiate the purpose of this bookcase from the ones in Susan's library, we removed all the contemporary fiction. After readjusting the shelves so that they were all evenly spaced, I created a pattern of art books by stacking them horizontally on the two center bottom shelves and all the way across the top three shelves. Next we arranged the leather-bound and first editions standing up on four of the remaining shelves.

In addition to the books, the shelves had also held several pieces of extremely fine pottery, a large piece of unpolished garnet that had been given to Susan by her brother, a couple of contemporary hand-hammered sterling-silver serving pieces, and, hidden on the very bottom shelves, three

artifacts in floating ebony-stained frames that I couldn't identify. As it turned out, these were actual bits of the Berlin Wall. So we moved them to the three center shelves at eye level, where they would be conspicuous enough for people to see them and ask about them. We moved two of the pottery pieces to the left and right bottom shelves, where they were clearly visible, and arranged the remaining pieces on higher shelves next to some of the leather-bound books.

To finish the room, I suggested that at some later date Susan add two more small paintings in gold-leaf frames to the four that were already on the wall to the left of the bookcase to give the entire assemblage more importance. The large Paul Henry painting was imposing enough to remain on the wall where it was by itself.

The room still doesn't look like a formal dining room, but all the seating now functions better, the dining table is more comfortably positioned so that traffic can flow more freely, and the artwork and accessories are displayed to their full potential. Except for adding the two paintings to the group next to the bookcase, my only other suggestion was that she adjust the overhead halogen lighting so that two of the spots would provide better illumination for the dining table.

THE CLIENT'S REACTION

It's extraordinary how changed the room is, particularly since we were able to do all this in less than an hour," Susan commented. "The whole space feels as if it's been dramatically transformed, but, in reality, it's only been subtly shifted, hasn't it?"

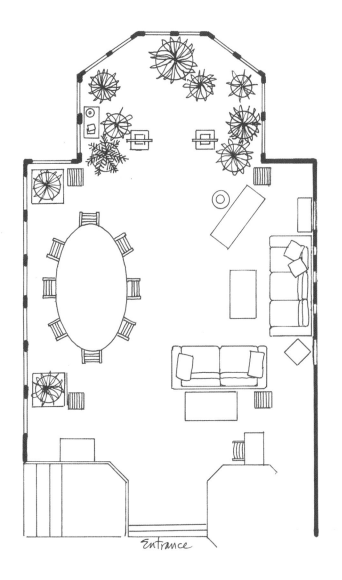

Entrance

Before　　She and her husband, Mikhail Baryshnikov, live in a lovely old house on a hill overlooking the Hudson River that he bought in 1981. Lisa and

Mikhail have been living there together since 1989. They have a son, Peter, fifteen, and two daughters, Ana, twelve, and Sophie, ten, as well as two dogs, two cats, and two birds.

The original house, although beautiful, hadn't been very large. As the children got bigger the space became smaller, so they built an enormous multipurpose room that they hoped would accommodate all of the family's activities. The problem, however, was that the room was so big—approximately 35 feet long by 23 feet wide—that it was overwhelming, and Lisa didn't know what to do to make the space seem welcoming and comfortable. As a result, the five of them still crammed themselves into the veranda to watch TV while the new space went to waste as a family gathering place.

The Diagnosis
THE FAMILY ROOM

The family room was really two rooms in one. At the near end, closest to the hallway and staircase that connected it to the older part of the house, was the

16

Making Bigger Better

REDESIGNING AN UNUSED EXTENSION

The Client and the Complaint

"I'm really exasperated," Lisa Rinehart greeted me as I walked in the door. "We spent so much money on this extension, thinking that it would solve our problem and we'd have the space we needed to spend our evenings together and be comfortable, but in fact we haven't made *any* changes to the way we use the house. It's very frustrating, and I really need help so that we can use this space." A ballet dancer with delicate features and beautiful blue eyes that were flashing her frustration, Lisa was at her wit's end.

Lisa Rinehart

seating area, which included a sofa and loveseat covered in the same striped country-style fabric. A lacquered wood and glass cocktail table with mirrored insets sat in front of the sofa. To the right of the sofa was a wrought-iron chaise lounge with a floral cushion that wasn't really a part of the conversation area. There were also two very nice, old wooden tables, one at the right end of the sofa and one behind the loveseat.

Architectural details, artwork, and accessories fought for attention in the conversation area of this handsome addition to the main house.

Before ▼

A lot of space was added to the Rinehart/ Baryshnikov house with this room, but it went virtually unused by the family.

Before ▲

Across from the sofa, closer to the windows, was a beautiful but enormous oak table with eight oak armchairs scattered around it and mirrored pedestals with plants on them at either end. The table was intended both for meals with guests and for doing vari-ous projects. (When I was there, it held Lisa's sewing machine.)

At the far end of the space, sepa-rated from the seating area by columns, was the garden room or atrium with double French doors leading to the garden. The ceiling in this part of the

180

room was about 20 feet high and sur-rounded at the top by a kind of bal-cony or catwalk that was accessed only from the floor above. The atrium was filled with plants and a pair of antique birdcages that held the family's ca-naries. "I wanted to fill it in somehow and make it look more homey and liv-able," Lisa said, "but it just doesn't feel right. Nothing feels right here."

As Lisa and I surveyed the room, I really liked the way it looked. The problem lay mainly with its function—or lack of it—rather than with the aes-thetics. One factor that we had to deal with was that there were almost no solid walls in any part of the space. The entire outer wall and the garden room were floor-to-ceiling windows, and the wall behind the sofa was also broken up with two large arched and three small square windows. Any room needs walls to anchor the furni-ture, and a room of that size could cer-tainly have benefited from having more walls than it did. Lisa's husband, Misha, had tried to give it more warmth by hanging a series of beauti-ful prints on what wall space was

available, but the effect, while attrac-tive, was busy rather than calming.

The challenge would be to tame the vastness so that the family could feel as warm and welcome there as they did on the veranda but with greater comfort.

The Mistakes
- Uncomfortable conversation area
- Improper use of artwork
- Ineffective use of accessories
- Improper lighting
- Lack of balance

The Remedy

There was, in fact, very little I could do to transform the family room that first day. It wasn't that the room didn't look attractive; it did. The basic prob-lem lay with the architecture. The good news was that it was very dra-matic; the bad news was that it was too overwhelmingly large to provide the cozy feeling the family had become accustomed to when they gathered on

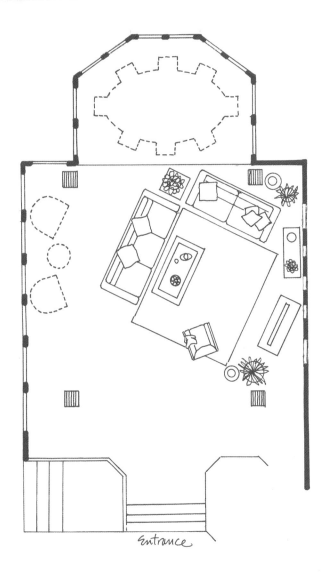

Entrance

After

plan that I believed would solve her problem.

The most important thing was to find a way to make the seating area more inviting for the family. To do that, I suggested that Lisa turn the sofa around so that its back would be to the wall of floor-to-ceiling windows and it would face the one solid wall (broken up though it was with windows) in the room. I recommended that she remove the decorative pots in the small square windows as well as the artwork Misha had hung above and below them. She could put a large flat-screen TV on that wall instead. The art was very beautiful, but the television would act as a lure for the family to gather. And, with the conversation area facing the wall rather than the large windows, the space would feel more cozy and inviting. In addition, if she had a media cabinet built in underneath the TV, they'd have a place to store their tapes, CDs, and DVDs.

Lisa could then position the loveseat perpendicular to the sofa so that it faced the stairway into the rest of the house and reupholster both the sofa and the loveseat in a solid-color che-

the veranda. All those windows, the stone floor, and the 20-foot-high ceiling in the atrium combined to make the space feel a bit cold and intimidating. But I was able to give Lisa a

nille that would be soft and comfortable. To complete and balance the conversation area, I suggested she purchase a club chair in the same height and style as that of the rest of the seating, perhaps in leather or a striped fabric. Although the coffee table was very attractive, the glass top was not very practical for putting your feet up and relaxing, but Lisa told me she had another one, with a wood top, in the guest house on the property, and I thought she should consider using that one instead.

To improve the light for reading as well as to create more balance, I recommended that she purchase a pair of lamps for the tables at either end of the sofa.

The problem with the oak table on the window side of the room was that the top was just too big. Since it was removable, I suggested that she store it and have a smaller, less overpowering one built. The table could then remain where it was or be moved so that it abutted the back of the sofa. I also recommended that she replace the mirrored pedestals with wooden ones, because the mirroring didn't seem to go with the country style of the rest of the furnishings.

And, finally, I suggested that she remove all the artwork from the walls to preserve the view and to give the eye a place to rest.

That still left the garden or atrium area at the back of the room. First of all, she needed to create a comfortable seating area so that people could actually use the space. At the moment, the only ones with a place to perch were the birds. I suggested a sofa in a solid fabric that picked up a color from the furnishings in the TV area, a chaise-type chair at either end, and a drum-shaped or square coffee table with rounded corners, or even a trunk in the middle. Throw pillows for the sofa in a coordinating fabric would also add to the coziness of the space.

Lisa didn't like the plants, so I recommended that she remove all of them except for one small palm tree and that she put a birdcage in front of each of the columns on the sunroom side to anchor them.

We also discussed the possibility of dropping the ceiling, eliminating the catwalk, and adding some halogen

◄ After

high hats for better light. The lower ceiling would give the family more room on the second floor and would make the garden room itself feel more cozy and comfortable. As it was, with so much glass and such high ceilings, sitting there actually made one feel a bit vulnerable and unprotected.

The Ultimate Result

When I returned several months later, the "garden" part of the family room was blocked floor-to-ceiling with heavy-duty plastic and filled with scaffolding. Workmen were in the process of dropping the ceiling and installing the lighting we'd discussed to make the space feel more intimate.

Although she'd done much of what we'd talked about, Lisa had tweaked the original design plan to make it her own. Rather than hanging a flat-screen TV on the wall beneath the small windows, she'd set it on top of a more compact media piece, catty-corner and closer to the stairs leading to the older part of the house. As we'd hoped, having the TV in the family room

at left: Careful editing of artwork and accessories and a more intimate conversation area made this room a real draw. It is now fulfilling the purpose for which it was built: a place for the family to come together.

185

HOME THERAPY

"I never would have thought of that!"

Turning the seating area around so that it faced the wall instead of the windows: "I was surprised that turning and 'enclosing' the TV area would make it feel more intimate," Lisa said.

proved to be the draw that got the family out of the veranda—and the room was already living up to its name.

Lisa had also purchased two tonsu chests, which she set one on top of the other on the wall nearest the arched window and just to the left of the television to hold the rest of the family's tapes and board games.

In addition, she'd bought a new sofa and loveseat and had them upholstered in burgundy-brown chenille with a bit of khaki woven through it. She'd also brought in a red and green upholstered chair from the formal living room. The chair was not as large as the one I'd envisioned to balance the size and weight of the other seating, but it worked well enough in the short term to complete the U-shaped conversation area.

The sofa now faces the wall with the loveseat perpendicular to it on the left and the chair on the right. The whole conversation area is anchored by a previously purchased rust, cream, and green rug that ties into the colors of the upholstery, although Lisa indicated to me that they might replace it with another similarly colored older one that they had in their city apartment. Both she and Misha prefer older things with lots of character.

Interestingly, although most of my female clients would choose aesthetics over function, whereas most males believe comfort is paramount, Lisa indicated that it was quite the opposite for her and Misha. "It makes me feel good when things function well," she told me. "Although I appreciate beauty, I like to be really comfortable. Misha really cares more than anything about how things look. He always wants to be more formal, and he loves things that have been used and lived with, even decaying. I think he was an aristocrat in his last life."

Knowing that, I had a chance to make a suggestion that I thought would please both of them when I saw that the original coffee table was still in place. Lisa told me that she'd tried another one, but it wasn't big or high enough to function properly in the space, so I recommended that she polyurethane the one she was using to preserve the lacquer finish and purchase three pieces of clear Lucite to put over the glass top to protect the mirrored insets. If she did that, people would be able to put their feet up and relax without worrying about breaking the glass or marring the table.

While I was there, we also brought in a pair of standing lamps from the formal living room to provide better task lighting and create more balance.

Most of the artwork was gone from the walls except for an oil painting Lisa loved, which we hung in the back corner above a large plant.

The sofa and loveseat were accessorized with throw pillows that picked up the colors in the rug and the chair, as did the thin wool throw on the arm of the chair itself.

On the coffee table we arranged a small harlequin puppet from Russia that Misha has had for many years, a "dancer" doll in a turquoise shirt that their son Peter had made, and a wooden bowl filled with apples. The tonsu chest held a Buddha that was a favorite of Lisa's standing on a painted box to raise it up and give it more prominence as well as a metal planter filled with greens and a small oil painting of fruit in a gold-leaf frame leaning against the wall.

In the end, we were both happy that we'd accomplished what we'd set out to do. By bringing in the large television and turning the furniture to face the wall rather than the long expanse of glass, the whole space felt cozier and more intimate. The room now worked; the family did gather there to watch television and videos, and Lisa told me that just a few days before, they'd had a sleepover with a large group of girls to celebrate both her daughters' birthdays, and the entire group had camped out on the floor. "Now that we're really using it," she said, "it's great to have such a large space."

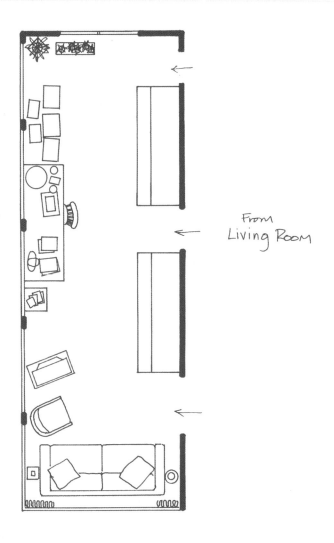

From
Living Room

Before

The multipurpose veranda was overcrowded with furniture and stuff. And while it was the main gathering place for the family to watch television, in addition to serving as an "office," it didn't accomplish either of these functions very well.

▲ Before

The Diagnosis
THE VERANDA

The veranda is a long, narrow room with full windows on three sides, all of which afford magnificent views of the countryside and river. A slipcovered sofa, rattan chair, ottoman, and television filled the space at one end of the room. In the middle, against the window wall, stood a desk overflowing with papers that held a Tiffany-style lamp, a bronze bust, and a contemporary task lamp. The desk was flanked by a white, two-drawer filing cabinet with a printer on top and boxes of papers.

Cluttered built-in bookcases with closed storage at the bottom filled the house wall of the room, and, at the farthest end of the room, where sliding glass doors led out to a porch, stood a tall plant stand beside a small blue painted planter.

The walls and curtains were sea foam green. The floor was done in a dramatic geometric patterned tile, which was predominately brown in color.

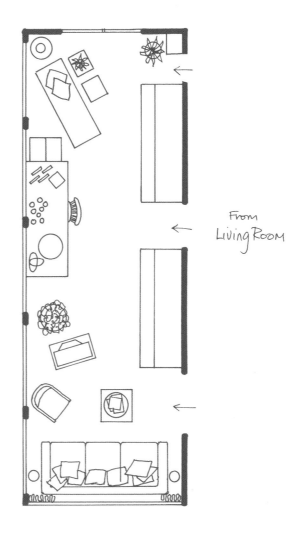

From Living Room

The Prescription

After

First, I recommended that Lisa replace the white sofa, which wasn't very comfortable or practical, with a more

189

comfortable piece in a darker color. Then she could redo the sea foam walls and curtains in an off-white. I also suggested that she purchase attractive wooden file cabinets (to replace the white file cabinet) that would match the stain on the desk. Next, I suggested she purge the bookcases of superfluous bric-a-brac and books the family no longer wanted or needed. Once she'd done that, she could rearrange the remaining books by size and pull them out to the edge of the shelves to create a "library" look. When the room was less messy and more comfortable, she might find that she and Misha were using it for purposes other than family TV and movie viewing.

Clearing away the clutter and using available furnishings and accessories more appropriately—without a huge investment—made this room far more attractive and functional.

The Ultimate Result

Within a few months, the veranda had been transformed. The walls had been repainted and the curtains replaced. In addition, Lisa had brought in the sofa from the family room and recovered it in a teal-colored cotton duck fabric.

After ▶

190

The conversation area is now complete with a matching ottoman and a natural rattan chair. A pair of brass swing-arm lamps with three-way bulbs at either end of the sofa provide good reading light.

The original TV is still there (although she will eventually replace it with a newer model), and, in the evening, Misha uses the veranda to watch the news or the golf tournaments he loves as well as to study tapes he brings home for his work.

The desk now has two wood file cabinets unobtrusively tucked side by side beneath its lip on the right. The clutter of papers is gone, leaving only a few family photos, *objets*, and a Tiffany lamp on top. And the bookcases are also cleared of their clutter, with the books arranged by size and subject: a whole section for books on ballet, another for books about Russia, and a collection of beautiful art books.

Lisa said that purging the excess from her home had been a wonderful experience that benefited her both aesthetically and psychologically. She now knows where everything is, and she uses the desk every day, both for tasks like paying household bills and for writing.

In the corner at the opposite end of the room, Lisa put the chaise from the family room, now recovered in a salmon-colored cotton that picks up the color in the tile floor, along with the beautiful old standing lamp with the painted shade that had been behind it. Although Lisa and I had talked about turning this into a spot where she could "get away" and relax quietly, she says that she doesn't have much time to relax, but the cats love to take their afternoon naps there.

So the veranda has not been abandoned in favor of the family room. Rather, both rooms are now fully functional and are being used in different ways, day and night.

"I never would have thought of that!"

Upholstering the sofa and ottoman in the same fabric: "I always had the notion that these two pieces should be different," said Lisa.

▲ After   The "office" area of the veranda now
enhances rather than detracts from the
rest of the room. And sitting at a well-
ordered desk, with such a magnificent
view of the countryside and river, makes
any task more pleasant.

THE CLIENT'S REACTION

It seemed clear that the changes I'd recommended and Lisa had made were benefiting the entire family.

"It's great that we can all watch a movie together and feel really comfortable now," Lisa exclaimed. "The first thing we noticed was that although the radiant heat from the floor warmed the room in winter, the furniture and rug were the things that made it feel comfy and cozy. The lighting made a big difference, too. Finally, we're actually using every room in the house!"

And, of course, the veranda is also more comfortable and inviting now than it was before. "It's functional in a way it never was," Lisa remarked. "I've always loved this room, but I was overwhelmed by the crazy floor pattern. Now it's relaxing to be in there because it isn't in chaos all the time. Things have become accessible."

17

Decorating Détente

PUTTING ALL THE PIECES TOGETHER, AT LONG LAST

The Clients and the Complaint

"I've been married a long time, and I'm really tired of having these battles with my husband about how we should do the space," Pamela Shearer said as she ushered me into her gracious center-hall colonial home. In fact, Pamela hadn't told her husband, Bruce, that I was coming. She'd already been "burned" (her word) by another sales-oriented designer, but she still wasn't entirely happy with how the place looked and was determined to get it together as quickly as possible.

Pamela and Bruce Shearer, with Cooper, haven't always agreed on how their home should look.

▼ Before ▶

The Shearers' living room hinted at a "decorator's" touch, but all the details didn't come together to make the room as elegant or as comfortable as they'd hoped.

Pamela, a stylish blonde, is a professor of sociology at a college in New York City and is currently writing a book about women who have left their careers to become full-time mothers. Bruce is the president of a nonprofit organization involved with international development. They have two sons, Alex and Nick, and a King Charles spaniel, Cooper.

It seemed that Alex's going off to college was the impetus for Pamela to finally get her home looking the way she wanted it to, but she wasn't really certain how to do that. Since the Use What You Have® philosophy is exactly the opposite of what she'd previously experienced, she turned to me for the help she knew she needed with the living room and dining room.

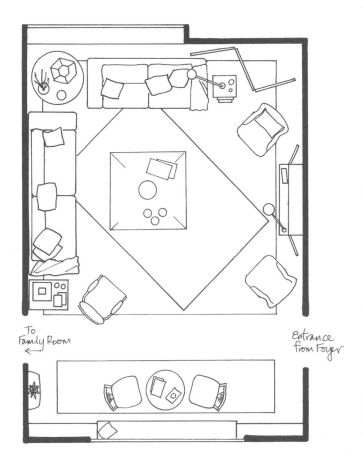

To Family Room ←

Entrance from Foyer

The Diagnosis
THE LIVING ROOM

The living room itself is graciously proportioned, approximately 21 feet long by 15 feet wide, with windows at either end facing the front and back of the house. At the back is a triple window with a built-in radiator cover that Pamela had cushioned to make a window seat. The problem, however, was that there was a loveseat—part of the L-shaped conversation area—directly in front of it, making the window seat,

Before

197

in effect, inaccessible and useless. The sofa was placed to the left of and perpendicular to the loveseat, with a large, round, glass-topped skirted table holding a tall lamp, a flower arrangement, and a crystal gazing ball in between. Pamela had slipcovered both pieces in khaki-colored cotton duck. She thought she had made a mistake, but they were actually quite attractive, although the configuration itself was uncomfortable. At the far end of the sofa, a small armchair upholstered in a

Beautiful pieces of furniture were not used as effectively as they might have been.

Before

tan and red dotted fabric was angled toward a large glass-and-metal cocktail table in the middle of the arrangement.

To the side of the sofa farthest from the window was a folding tray table with a tall, narrow, ebony wood lamp with a persimmon-colored pagoda-shaped shade. At the other end of the loveseat there was a step table with a black metal long-necked reading light. Behind it, at an angle and cutting off the corner, was a plain beige linen screen.

The wall opposite the sofa was dominated by a large, painted, cherry wood antique secretary with a blue interior, which Pamela had accessorized with a gold-leaf tray holding a crystal decanter and some glasses, some pottery, and other bits and pieces. On either side of it she'd placed matching lady chairs covered in dark camel and white buffalo-checked material. Very beautiful but also very high, the secretary created a roller-coaster effect by causing the eye to go up to the top, then down to the chair, then up again to the screen.

The area was anchored by a neutral-colored sisal area rug that had a smaller Aubusson rug in shades of mocha, tan, and blue with rose-colored flowers on the border angled on top of it. Although the smaller rug was very pretty, I thought that it was redundant—like wearing a jacket over a coat—and that it chopped up the space.

At the opposite end of the room at the front of the house is a lovely double window with a proper window seat in front of which stood a beautiful, round, burled-wood table and a pair of Hepplewhite shield-back chairs. A patterned sisal rug ran parallel to the windows under the table and chairs. There were built-in bookcases with closed storage beneath on either side of the windows. On the wall perpendicular to the windows was a small cabriole-legged gold-leaf table holding a vase of flowers and above it a painting.

Pamela has a good eye and had been instinctively seeking cohesion. She had, for example, made throw pillows for the sofa and loveseat that had needlepoint centers with a border of the dotted fabric from the small uphol-stered chair. She'd taken the blue for the Aubusson rug from the blue interior of the secretary and had also found a blue bowl, which she filled with red porcelain balls, for the coffee table.

On the wall above the sofa she'd hung a painting that had belonged to her mother. She said that Bruce hated the frame, but so far they hadn't done anything about it. In fact, she had some very lovely things, but they were scattered about the room and not being shown as effectively as they could have been.

The Living Room Mistakes

- Improper furniture placement
- Uncomfortable conversation area
- Poorly lit room
- Ineffective use of accessories
- Lack of balance
- Lack of cohesion

Shifting the large secretary off the long wall made for a more comfortable and accessible conversation area while balancing the weight of the off-center window.

After ▲

The Remedy

We started by rearranging the furniture and accessories for an instant change. The first thing to go was the Aubusson rug, which Pamela would use in another room. Then we removed the screen and put the secretary on the back wall to the right of the triple window, where its weight would be better balanced by the weight of the window. The screen itself wasn't particularly decorative, and it, too, would go into another room.

Now that the long wall was free of the secretary, we swung the loveseat around to face the sofa, a few inches out from the wall. Doing that not only created a more comfortable conversation area (because those seated would now be able to face one another) but also revealed the window seat and made it available for use.

I brought in the very lovely oval black-lacquer container I'd seen by the hearth in the dining room, and put it at the side of the loveseat farthest from the window with some books on top. Behind it we placed a pharmacy lamp that had been in a bedroom and, to the side, a small ficus tree to fill in and soften the wall.

Above the loveseat, just to the left of the lacquer container, we took four small prints in matching bamboo

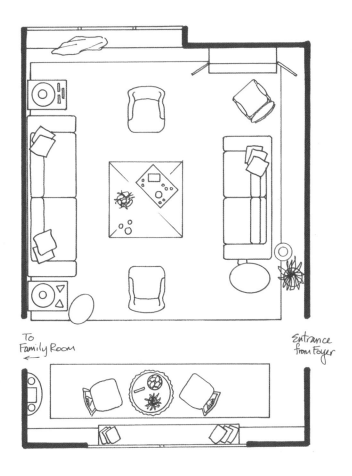

To Family Room ←

Entrance from Foyer

After

201

The use of pairs throughout the room
goes a long way toward achieving a
well-balanced and harmonious feeling.

After ▲

frames that pick up the wood tone of the secretary and hung them vertically, with the smallest on top. We left the rest of that wall blank, giving the eye a place to rest, and left the painting that had belonged to Pamela's mother above the sofa, which was actually the right place for it.

We put the small upholstered chair next to the secretary, where Pamela could sit to write a note, and I used the niches in the upper section to display a collection of old leather-bound books and several sterling-silver accessories.

We moved the sofa a few inches into the room so that anyone seated on it wouldn't have to raise his or her voice in order to converse easily with those on the loveseat. Both could make use of the coffee table between them. To complete the conversation area we put the two buffalo-checked lady chairs at either end, creating an intimate circle.

We replaced the skirted table in the corner with the step table. We left the tray table in place at the opposite end of the sofa and stacked a few books on top to equalize its height with that of the step table. Now the two wooden end tables are of much more equal height and weight. In the family room I found a pair of off-white ginger jar lamps with linen shades that would be perfect for the tables. These lamps had three-way bulbs, which provide better lighting than the lamps with 60-watt bulbs that had been there, which would move to other rooms.

On the coffee table, along with a trio of carved wooden candlesticks, we created a display of painted Russian boxes that I'd found scattered about the house, arranging them on a large, black lacquer tray.

At the front end of the room, we replaced the burled-wood table in front of the bay window with the skirted one that had been in the back corner. The table and chairs were rather leggy; the skirted table added more weight to balance the weight at the other end of the room. The flower arrangement that had originally been on the table remained, and to it we added a bowl filled with some wonderful stone eggs that had been in the family room and a hand-painted tile on a stand.

Accessories gathered from all parts of the room, well displayed, give each arrangement importance without detracting from the beautiful furniture or the architectural details.

▲ After

Then we folded down one of the drop leaves of the burled table and stood it against the wall where the smaller gold-leaf table had been. The burled table is a much larger, more important-looking piece, especially once we accessorized it with Pamela's grandmother's clock and a pair of candlesticks, all of which had been in a bedroom. Finally, we put a few throw pillows on the window seat to make it more inviting and to pick up the colors in the table skirt and the fabric of the shield-back chair cushions.

Simply by rearranging the furniture, all of which had been in the room to begin with, and gathering accessories that had been scattered throughout the house, we created a much more comfortable and functional space that also showed off the things Pamela and Bruce loved.

Long-Term Recommendations

I recommended that when and if Pamela decided to repaint the living room, she use a dark tan color for the

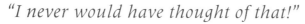

"I never would have thought of that!"

Using so many of the things Pamela and Bruce had collected or inherited—including the painted Russian boxes together with the black lacquer tray, the Japanese container, and the clock—in ways she had never imagined.

walls to pick up the color in the buffalo-checked chairs, and, if she did that, she could replace the off-white shades on the lamps with pure white ones to brighten the room.

Because the secretary isn't quite as high as the top of the triple window, I suggested that she purchase a long, flat planter to put on top and fill it with ivy to equalize the heights.

Since Bruce really disliked the frame of the painting over the sofa, I recommended that she have it redone in a larger, more dramatic wood frame with some gold leaf on it.

Beyond that, my only remaining suggestions were that she reframe all the family photos in silver and display them on the step table, that she cover the topsoil of the ficus plant with Spanish moss for a more finished look, and that she purchase a few throw pillows, preferably in blue and off-white, for the sofa and loveseat.

The Diagnosis
THE DINING ROOM

When we got to the dining room Pamela confessed, "It just doesn't look the way I want it to. It's not that I want to buy new furniture; I just know it can look better." And, in fact, the problems she perceived in the dining room really were all about accessories.

The walls were painted a dramatic Chinese red. The Elizabeth Eakins gold and white–checked rug is quite lovely. The white-painted dining table and chairs have a lot of style, and the woven, small, leopard-print seat cushions are eye-catching. In the near right-hand corner by the entrance to the room was a narrow secretary that served as a bar. At the back of the room under a high horizontal window stood a beautiful, marble-topped mahogany server. The centerpiece, a

205

serene Buddha, which is a favorite of Bruce's, sat in front of a Japanese silk-screened piece of art. There were also two white candlestick lamps, two white porcelain candlesticks, and a few other accessories. The crystal chandelier over the table is very nice, but the light from the bare bulbs was harsh.

The large windows had off-white curtains with gold stars that hung on gold poles with rings. On the opposite wall is a working fireplace whose man-

Before ▼

Handsome architectural details, fine furnishings, and the rich Chinese red color on the walls were an excellent start to transform this dining room into something really dramatic.

tel was decorated with a round mirror in a square gold-leaf frame made up of circles radiating outward and a couple of topiaries, one larger than the other. On the hearth were some fireplace tools and a basket of wood as well as the black lacquer container.

A large piece of beige pottery holding branches stood in the rear right corner of the room but didn't appear to be doing much of anything either practically or decoratively.

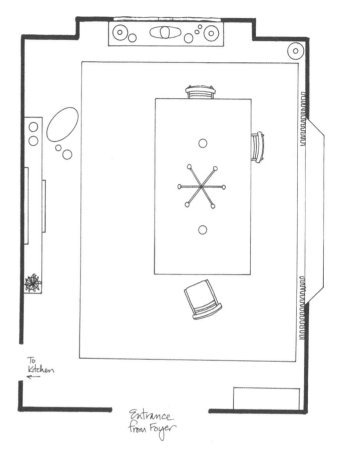

Before

The Dining Room Mistakes

- Ineffective use of accessories
- Improper use of artwork
- Badly lit room

The Remedy

Pamela had said that she didn't want to buy new furniture, and, in fact, there was absolutely no reason to do so. We did collect the remaining dining chairs from various rooms and reunite them around the table. Beyond that, however, all the room really needed was to be put together in a way that would give it more drama and cohesion.

The Buddha and candlestick lamps remained on the server, but we brought the lamps forward a bit. From a cupboard, Pamela brought out a pair

207

of white candles banded with gold, which we put in the brass candlesticks that had been on the dining table and stood them on the server to the left and right of the Buddha. Then we took the smaller topiary from the fireplace mantel, found its mate, and put them on either side of the server along with a smaller pair that had also been on the mantel. To complete the display, we switched the Japanese silk screen, which had previously been hidden behind the Buddha, with the mirror that had been on the mantel. With the mirror behind the Buddha, it now looks as if the gold-leaf circles are radiating around him. The entire arrangement is now very peaceful and beautiful.

The Japanese silk screen was perfect on the mantel, where it is now flanked by the two large topiaries as well as by two very beautiful pitchers, one of which had been on top of the server and the other stored inside. To complete the fireplace arrangement, we found a narrow, black lacquer and bamboo box with a brass latch that was just the right size to hold the two fire starters that had been standing on the hearth.

Everything that was needed to make this room really dramatic was already there; it just needed the "decorator" touch that had eluded the Shearers.

After ▶

208

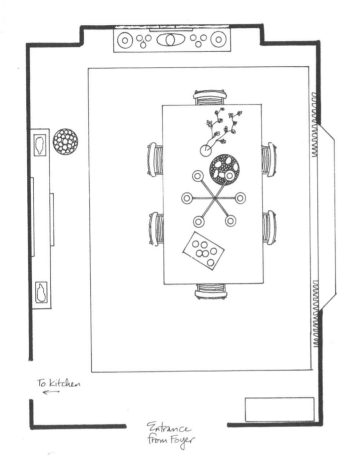

To kitchen

Entrance
from Foyer

After

On the dining table itself, we placed the blue bowl with the red porcelain balls that had been on the cocktail table in the living room, adding a few fresh lemons so that the bright colors really popped. Next to that we placed the gold-leaf tray with the decanter and glasses from the secretary in the living room, along with an oversized sterling-silver martini shaker, which had been on the dining room bar, and an orchid plant.

Long-Term Recommendations

To redirect the light from the chandelier downward and get rid of the shadows it cast, I recommended that Pamela purchase small silk clip-on shades for the bulbs.

For the windows, I suggested that she buy gold and ruby tiebacks for the curtains as well as gathered sheers on top and bottom poles to go all the way across the bottom windows, which would provide a sense of privacy at night.

The only additional accessory I thought she should have was a large oxblood porcelain pot to hold the firewood on the hearth.

"I never would have thought of that!"

Placing the Japanese silk screen on the mantel and the gold-leaf mirror behind the Buddha: Each works so much better in its new place, and the mirror really makes the arrangement with the Buddha so much more dramatic.

The Ultimate Result

Although my return visit—to help Pamela redecorate the family room and master bedroom suite—was less than two weeks following our initial meeting because she and Bruce would be leaving the following day to drive Alex to college, she had already accomplished an enormous amount.

In the living room, the painting had not yet been reframed, but the box with the ivy was in place above the secretary. Pamela had added a silver vase filled with sunflowers to the display on the coffee table. She'd also found two blue and two off-white ultrasuede throw pillows for the sofa, a beautiful blue chenille throw for the back window seat, and a couple of pillows that were blue with off-white chrysanthemums on one side and the

reverse on the other, all of which acknowledged the blue of the secretary.

The photos had been reframed and were displayed, as I'd suggested, on the step table, and she'd added a basket filled with magazines under the tray table.

On a trip to the powder room that day, I discovered three white-painted metal birds, garden ornaments that had belonged to Pamela's grandmother. She loved the birds and so did I, so I arranged them on the tray table—one on top of the books and the other two looking at it—so that the three of them are now looking at one another.

In the dining room, she'd purchased the silk shades for the chandelier, the tiebacks for the curtains, the gathered white sheers for the bottom windows, and the pot for the wood.

A few added details and a little
refinement really brought this
room to life.

THE CLIENTS' REACTION

As we were working on the day of my first visit, Pamela exclaimed, "It's like a puzzle; you're making the most of what I've got. In fact, it's really more than what I've got." And, as we finished the dining room, she said, "You've given me what I've always wanted but couldn't get. I love the way you used the Asian pieces. It's not too heavy, and my husband is going to be thrilled."

Bruce arrived home shortly thereafter. Pamela and I waited until we heard him say "Wow!" Then he turned to us, eyebrows raised, and looked into the dining room: "Amazing!" At that point Pamela broke out into a huge smile, and Bruce, somewhat impishly, turned to me and said, "You know, I'm not easy when it comes to decorating, but this is absolutely amazing. I can't get over it."

The next day, I received this e-mail: "Bruce and I have been sitting around here oohing and aahing and marveling at the amazing transformation to our rooms since you left. We can't get over the dramatic changes."

18
Preparing for Baby and Buyers

GETTING RESALE-READY™

The Clients and the Complaint

"What can I do with this place to make it more attractive to potential buyers without having to invest a fortune? I feel that I really need to work quickly before my pregnancy is so far along that I won't be able to get around easily."

Those were the words with which Melissa Secrest greeted me at the door to the spacious home she shares with her husband, Mark. She's a Ph.D. candidate in psychotherapy and he is a banker, and I was immediately struck

Melissa Secrest

Before ▲

by the fact that in all the photographs I saw of them in their home, they looked as if they were laughing and having a wonderful time together. When I met them, they were expecting a baby in four months and thought that some time in the not too distant future they would be moving to larger quarters in a more child-friendly neighborhood. In the meantime, however, they wanted to make their current home as appealing as possible, not only for the potential buyer but also for themselves, without spending too much money on permanent fixtures or architectural alterations.

As it happens, Melissa called because she had heard about the Resale-Ready™ Redecorating service offered at Use What You Have® and by the Interior Refiners Network®. While we always explain to our clients that any suggestions we make are geared to increasing the value of their home—whether or not they are planning to move—we can also transform rooms simply and inexpensively for those who want to sell quickly or maximize their potential resale price, which is what we did for the Secrests that day.

◄ Before

The living/dining area in this loftlike space has a lot of character. But even with lots of attractive furnishings, interesting art, and artifacts, things didn't look pulled together.

217

The Diagnosis

Melissa wanted me to work specifically on the living and dining areas, which were really one large open space differentiated from one another by the placement of the furniture. Although it was perfectly clear that the section of the room closest to the open kitchen, which was furnished with a very nice, midcentury table and black leather chairs, was the dining area, there were other furnishings and accessories in that part of the room that really belonged in the living room and vice versa.

Against the brick wall at the back of the dining area, there was a high Baker wall unit with sixteen cube-shaped openings holding a variety of accessories that looked like it really belonged in a living room. Conversely, at the far end of the living room, against a second exposed-brick wall, the Secrests had placed a curved modern marble-topped black wood console table with steel legs and trim that was holding their audio equipment but would have functioned much better as a sideboard in the dining area.

Also in the dining area on a narrow wall between two windows was a large African landscape photo by Peter Beard. Beneath some smaller photos hanging to the right of the wall unit were one dining chair and a tiny telephone table. A dracaena and two corn plants, one of which was much too large for the space, sat in the corner near a window. The large oriental rug under the table and chairs anchored the entire area.

The living room was separated from the dining area by a long pine console holding a large Chinese ginger jar, a very pretty cloisonné lamp without a shade that had belonged to Melissa's grandmother, and a tray with a small selection of liquor. A doubled-trunked corn plant stood between the console and the window.

A sofa covered in raspberry chenille was backed up against the console on the living room side, facing the far end of the room. There was a large leather ottoman serving as a cocktail table in front of the sofa, and a club chair covered in the same raspberry chenille fabric next to a potted tree facing the sofa along the window wall. On the other side of the chair stood a square wooden end table with three open-tiered shelves that held a pewter lamp with a black paper shade as well as a few art books and accessories. A second oriental rug that blended very well with the one in the dining area anchored the whole conversation area.

Except for a couple of floor pillows, the rest of the room was bare all the way to the back wall. In the back corner, on the window side of the console, there was a 4-foot-high black speaker. Its mate, along with a 6-foot-high wine vault, stood on the opposite side of the console. The windows, which ran down the length of one wall, had old Roman shades. The windowsills, which were covered by a long oak built-in window seat that housed the central heating and air-conditioning unit, were cluttered with a variety of bric-a-brac.

In fact, Melissa was correct when she said that she felt the space wasn't pulled together, but it wouldn't be difficult to change that feeling almost at once.

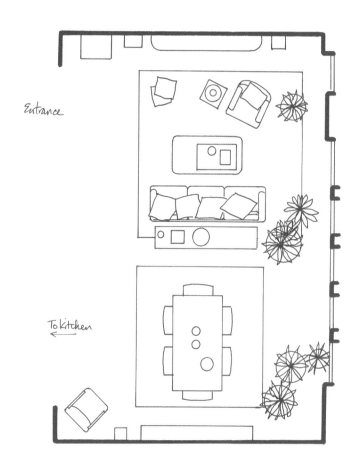

The Mistakes

Before

- Poor furniture placement
- Lack of cohesion
- Lack of balance
- Incorrect use of artwork
- Ineffective use of accessories

The Remedy

Correcting the mistakes in the dining area took less than an hour. The first thing we did was to remove all the accessories from the cubes of the wall unit and to move the unit itself to the far end of the living room. We also moved the living room console to the dining area, where it would be much more useful. We then shifted the table and chairs a bit closer to the back wall and reunited with its mates the single dining room chair that had been floating next to the telephone table.

We removed the three smaller photos and replaced them with the Peter Beard photo over the console. A small, square, red oil painting that had been virtually lost on the brick wall in the living room found a new home on the console below the Beard, where it picked up the splotch of red from the photo. A pair of small lamps that had been in the bedroom, where they didn't provide enough reading light, now served to balance and complete the display on the console.

The small telephone table remained where it was because it was easily accessible. We did, however, move the large corn plant from the corner near the window to the living room, where it joined a smaller one next to the club chair. We replaced it with the corn plant that had been next to the center console by the window, which was a much better size and shape for the space.

To complete the change, we removed the accessories from the dining table and placed the drinks tray that had been on the pine console at an angle on the end farthest from the wall so that it wouldn't interfere with family dinners and could easily be removed when there was company. And finally, the three large white candles, which had been grouped in a semicircle, were lined up down the center instead.

The area immediately looked more of a piece, with better balance and cohesion of the furnishings and a much more effective use of artwork and accessories.

Careful editing of accessories and effective use of available furnishings make a huge difference. Pieces now feel balanced and the whole space has a cleaner, more sophisticated look.

After ▶

220

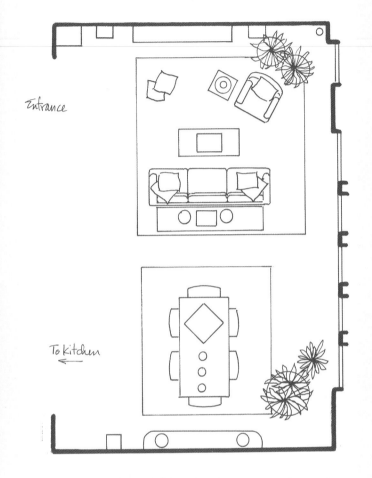

Entrance

To kitchen

After

> The large wall unit was much more effective in the living area, where it was more visible and made a more dramatic statement than the smaller, lighter console had. We rearranged the accessories in the six-

teen cube openings according to category. The top row, for example, held only African masks.

I found a narrow dark brown leather tufted ottoman in the bedroom that worked much better as a coffee table than the one the Secrests had been using. And, in fact, the larger ottoman worked much better in the bedroom. Switching the two pieces actually improved both areas at once.

We removed the audio equipment but left the speakers flanking the wall unit. The wine cooler was shifted a bit farther into the corner along with the taller of the two corn plants from the dining room and a shorter, wider plant. Not only did they partially conceal the white pipe that ran floor to ceiling in the corner, but they also balanced one another nicely to create a dramatic statement.

Finally, we removed all the objects that had been cluttering the windowsills and changed the accessories that had been on the wooden console behind the sofa. In the kitchen, I found a beautiful antique wedding box to place in the center, where it not only looked attractive but also could be used to store a variety of bits and pieces. I flanked the box with a pair of pedestal marble balls that had previously been in the family room. While the pieces that had been there were of various heights and unrelated to one another, creating a disconcerting roller-coaster effect, the new display was much cleaner and more balanced.

The living and dining areas were now two distinct spaces, and both were more cohesive, better balanced, and generally more pulled together.

Long-Term Recommendations

To finish the new look in the dining room, I recommended that the Secrests replace the three hanging lights above the table, which were too low, with a single fixture to hold three halogen spotlights. Alternatively, they could clip the ends of the existing track, which was too long, and replace the three white hanging fixtures with three adjustable halogen lights.

I also suggested that they stain and polyurethane the floors and remove the dining area rug to further separate and delineate the two spaces, not to mention making after-dinner cleanups a lot easier, especially after the baby's birth.

To complete the conversation area, I suggested that the Secrests purchase a second chair in a fabric to match the club chair or in a solid navy or pea green to pick up the colors in the living room rug. A pair of pharmacy lamps to improve the lighting at either

"I never would have thought of that!"

Flipping the dining room display unit with the living room console: This simple exchange made the room look and work better.

end of the sofa would also be in order.

The Roman shades were in need of replacement, so I suggested linen semi-opaque Duette shades with a top-down option, which would look much cleaner and provide privacy without obscuring the northern light or the view.

Because details often make an important difference, I recommended that they purchase three matching ceramic pots to hold the three trees and that they cover the top of the soil with Spanish moss for a neater, more finished look.

Painting the walls linen white in an eggshell or flat finish, with the trim in semigloss, and painting the window unit the same color with a couple of coats of polyurethane on the top would further enhance the appearance of the space while the family remained in residence and at the same time make it more attractive to a buyer. I also suggested that they consider painting the white pipe in the far corner terracotta, to blend into the brick wall behind it.

◄ After

at left: Bringing complementary pieces and accessories together made a big difference in both the look and function of the space. In particular, the placement of the console, with the pair of lamps framing the large photo, created a practical, dramatic focal point in the dining area.

THE CLIENT'S REACTION

When I moved the small red painting in the dining area, Melissa told me how fond she was of it and how delighted she was that it could now be seen to its full advantage. When we were done, she was equally excited to see how much we'd been able to do so quickly simply by moving a few pieces of furniture. "This is incredible," she remarked. "I just love the way the art looks and everything seems to fit the space better. And we haven't spent any money at all!"

She also understood that painting walls and refinishing or repairing floors are improvements she couldn't take with her when the family moved but were important and fairly economical when one considered their value for resale.

19
Easy Listening

LIVING WITH A VERY GRAND PIANO

The Client
and the Complaint

"I just don't like this room," Naomi Sinnreich said bluntly. "I have no storage. It doesn't look right, and it isn't comfortable either for us as a family or when I entertain." A retired corporate attorney, Naomi has been married to a physician for twenty-nine years and is the mother of two teenage daughters, Elizabeth and Michelle. She'd been referred to Use What You Have® when she began complaining about the space to a neighbor who had read my books, and now she let me know that, as far as she was concerned, everything in the living room except the piano could go.

Naomi Sinnreich at her beloved piano.

Playing her Steinway grand is her passion and has been ever since she was a young woman, when she contemplated becoming a professional musician. Now, she still takes lessons and plays for pleasure. In fact, she gives her music so much time and attention that her daughter Michelle told me the piano was like her third child.

In addition to being dedicated to her music, however, I could tell that Naomi was extremely detail oriented and a perfectionist in whatever she set her mind to, and that she would make it her mission to "get the room right."

The Diagnosis

The 20 by 11–foot living room, which is two steps down from the entrance and the dining room, is fairly spacious

and well proportioned, but because of the way the furniture was arranged it appeared cluttered and busy rather than attractive and peaceful. "Your room isn't a true reflection of who you are," I told Naomi. "You are an elegant woman, and you should have an elegant room."

The piano was on the long left wall, close to the entrance and angled slightly toward the middle of the room. On the same wall was a very long (98-inch) sofa upholstered in a blue, pink, and white floral pattern. Beyond it was a standing lamp, and, in the corner on the window wall, was a small wood cabinet with a sculpture of a man on top of it. Also hanging on this wall were three different paintings in three different framing materials.

The south-facing windows were hung with sheer white curtains and roller shades, and there was an air conditioner in the window to the right. Centered in front of the windows Naomi had placed a glass and wood end table with a plant and, in front of that two side-by-side barrel chairs perpendicular to the far end of the sofa and facing into the room. To

This living room was a jumble of furniture in need of a good plan to make it look and feel better.

Before ▶

the right of the window was a Chinese porcelain plant stand holding another plant. The U-shaped seating arrangement was completed with two wooden Chippendale-style chairs facing the barrel chairs. There was no coffee table and thus no place for anyone seated on either the sofa or the chairs to put anything down. The entire conversation area was anchored by a 9 by 12–foot dhurrie rug in shades of pink and blue. Above the seating hung a track with several large can lights.

Lined up along the right-hand wall from the entranceway to the window were a small bookcase, an executive-style desk with a desk lamp and a basic wooden chair, a tall, 98-inch-long wall unit in white lacquer and glass that held a variety of silver, dishes, and other collectibles, and, finally, an industrial metal plant stand covered in grow lights.

Not only was there a lot going on in the room, but the piano was effectively obstructing the traffic pattern to the seating area, and the furniture of different heights pushed up against the walls all around was creating a disconcerting roller-coaster effect.

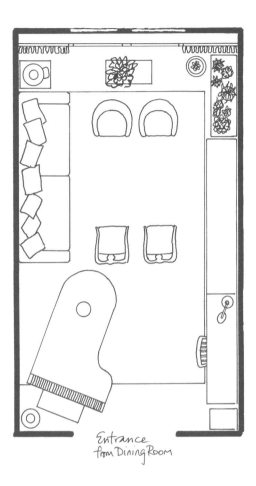

Entrance from Dining Room

The Mistakes

- Poor furniture placement
- Uncomfortable conversation area
- Awkward traffic pattern
- Furniture of different heights
- Badly lit room
- Improper use of artwork
- Ineffective use of accessories
- No focal point

Before

229

The Remedy

As sometimes happens when I'm called in to consult with a client, there was little that I could do that day to immediately reconfigure and transform the room. What I did do was to provide Naomi with a detailed design plan for her to follow in order to make the changes we discussed.

Although the room has good light, the view from the windows isn't particularly interesting or attractive. Since one of Naomi's key concerns was that she have adequate storage, I suggested that she cover the entire window wall with a shoji screen. Behind it, on either side of the windows, she could then build floor-to-ceiling shelving that would be completely hidden by the screen. Even though the screen remained closed, there would be light streaming in through the translucent rice paper. She could even incorporate a drop-down panel in one of the rice-paper boxes to expose the air conditioner when it was in use without opening the entire screen.

To improve the traffic pattern and create a dramatic focal point, I suggested centering the piano, with its straight side facing the window and its graceful curve facing into the room, on the window wall.

Despite the fact that Naomi was more than willing to dispose of all her furniture (except, of course, the piano), I recommended that she keep and simply reupholster the barrel chairs, which were both basic and comfortable. For more comfort and better feng shui, I proposed moving the conversation area to the wall to the right of the entrance. With a new, smaller sofa along the wall and the two barrel chairs separated and placed facing one another at either end, she'd still have a comfortable U shape, and

"I never would have thought of that!"

Covering the entire window wall with a shoji screen and creating floor-to-ceiling storage behind it: Naomi was initially a bit doubtful that there would be a simple and elegant solution to all her needs—comfortable seating, adequate storage, and display space—but the suggestion of the full wall screen and storage changed her opinion.

the seating would be clearly visible from the entrance, inviting people into the room. Since she needed a new sofa, I recommended that she look for one that was comfortable and have it upholstered in a fabric incorporating the burgundy and neutral colors she told me she liked. As it happened, she had a photo of a sofa she'd already ordered that fit my description. Now she could look for a new rug in those colors, or, if she wanted more coverage for the wood floor, she could buy solid-color carpeting and have it cut to look like a rug with a self-binding, leaving a border of wood all around the room.

To complete the conversation area, I suggested a round or oval coffee table and a pair of end tables incorporating closed storage for either end of the sofa as well as a pair of ginger jar–style table lamps in oxblood red (with three-way bulbs, of course) and ivory silk shades.

For the left wall opposite the sofa, I recommended that she look for a piece that would accommodate both display and storage and that she use the display portion for only her best pieces of

Entrance from Dining Room

non-food-related silver because, as I explained, accessories generally should be kept in the room where they're most appropriate.

To finish things off, I proposed painting the walls, which had been a blue gray, in deep cream or soft white with the trim and ceiling in Super White. The track that she already had

After

231

didn't need to be replaced, but I did suggest that she get tiny halogen spots to replace the large old-fashioned cans for general illumination.

The Ultimate Result

I knew Naomi was eager to carry out the plan I'd given her, and I anticipated her being a stickler for details, but when I returned, even I was stunned by the complete transformation the room had undergone. It's true, of course, that the change is more dramatic when a room is totally redone than it is when existing furniture and artwork are simply rearranged. Nevertheless, it was obvious that Naomi hadn't been kidding when she said she would "make it her mission" to get it right.

She'd followed every one of my recommendations for furniture placement, and the pieces she'd found were all perfect. The screen was in place, the piano had been moved, and the room now had an elegant and compelling focal point.

The sofa she found has comfortable loose pillows and rounded arms and is upholstered in taupe chenille with specks of burgundy. The barrel chairs have been reupholstered in solid wine chenille, and Naomi has put them on brass casters, as I'd suggested, for flexibility, which, as it happened, also raises them up so that they are more closely aligned with the height of the sofa.

Her coffee table is a lovely mahogany oval with two shelves below and is a perfect size for the room. On top is a Lalique glass sculpture that had formerly been on the piano along with a couple of art books and a vase of fresh flowers.

As I'd recommended, she found two Chinese cabinets with closed storage to use as end tables and a pair of oxblood lamps that are narrow enough for the small tables.

The display piece she'd found is an absolutely gorgeous mahogany and glass deco-style breakfront with brass handles and drawers underneath. Based on what I'd suggested and what she'd read in my books, she had beautifully arranged her favorite silver pieces behind the glass doors.

Opposite: It is hard to believe that this is the same room. But the clever use of a full-wall shoji screen was the first step in a dramatic transformation that made the piano the centerpiece of the room without overwhelming it.

◄ After

233

The only artwork remaining on the walls are two similar brass-framed pieces hanging one above the other on the left-hand wall on the window side of the breakfront. And over the sofa she'd hung an Asian screen in colors that complement her fabrics. When she showed it to me on my first visit, she told me that she'd purchased it on a whim and had never found the right place to hang it. As it happened, the screen is not only a lovely decorative piece, but it also helps to balance the height of the breakfront on the other side of the room.

In the near corner on the left, instead of the bulk of the piano there is a small stone water fountain. And past the breakfront, on the same wall, is a very pretty pedestal with a gold-leaf porcelain vase in which Naomi keeps fresh flowers.

Where previously there had been a clutter of furniture in disparate sizes and styles that made the room appear too busy for comfort, there are now clean, elegant, almost Asian lines. To give the room a more spacious feeling, Dr. Sinnreich has sacrificed his large metal plant stand, and the executive desk was removed because Naomi has one in her study.

THE CLIENT'S REACTION

Can you believe this is the same room?" Naomi exclaimed when I returned to see the transformation she'd completed. "Until I met you, no one had the right vision for the room. Every other decorator had the same tired ideas about window treatments, but your suggestion for the shoji screens solved all my problems. Now I can't imagine how I ever lived without them. I have great storage, and it's very calming and soothing.

"I followed all your suggestions for the room, and now I love it," she concluded. But while it was true that I'd provided the design plan and she had, indeed, followed it to the letter, it was also obvious that the room now finally reflected her own passion and personality.

20
Artist in Residence

LONGTIME ART COLLECTORS TAKE STOCK

The Clients and the Complaint

"My husband and I love the light and the view from our living room, but it doesn't really feel comfortable to us, and I've never quite known where to put all my sculpture. As a result, we spend most of our time in the sunroom, and that just seems silly to me."

Helen and Bernard Sokolov have been married for more than fifty years. He is a retired builder and developer, and she is a talented artist who paints in oils and sculpts in stone. Having raised two daughters in a suburban house, they had moved to their spa-

Helen and Bernard Sokolov

cious city apartment six years before I met them.

Their furnishings are modern, and the artwork throughout is abundant. In fact, the artwork, scattered throughout the living room, was the first thing I noticed upon entering. Despite the grand size and decor of the apartment, however, the Sokolovs had been feeling uncomfortable in what should have been a sumptuous, elegant, and functional space. Bernard couldn't find a cozy corner where he could settle comfortably to read, and they both found their living room an uncomfortable place to entertain. Neither of them was as happy in their home as they both thought they could be.

Before ▼

Before ▲

The Diagnosis

Despite the quality and abundance of their artwork and Helen's undeniable talent and artistic knowledge, one of the biggest mistakes I discovered in the Sokolovs' apartment was their improper use of artwork and accessories.

After more than fifty years together, the Sokolovs had a lifetime of collecting to deal with. Fortunately, this large, well-proportioned room would be able to accommodate virtually everything they wanted.

237

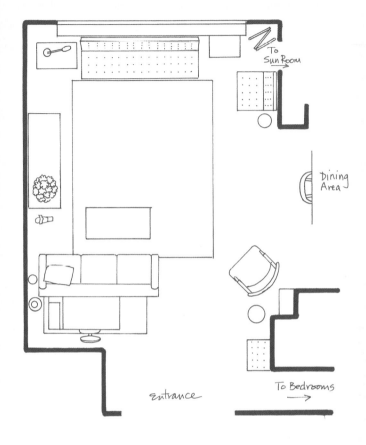

Before

Everywhere I turned there was something to look at, so that the view from the windows, which was truly spectacular and should have been the primary focal point, had to fight for whatever attention it could get. It was impossible for the eye to rest there for any length of time before being pulled in another direction. Rather than feeling calmed by the surroundings, I was distracted by sensory overload.

A second, equally important source of discomfort was the arrangement of the living room furniture. It's no wonder the couple found their living room a difficult place in which to entertain. Although the room was certainly large enough, and the seating more than adequate, the two large sofas that composed the main conversation area were so far apart that one would have had to shout across the vast expanse of oriental carpet to be heard. The coffee table in front of the sofa nearest to the entrance was totally inaccessible to those on the second sofa, and two additional chairs were pushed back against the wall and so far into the corners that they might as well have been in a different room.

The furniture placement not only made conversation difficult, if not impossible, it also obstructed entrance into the room and created a poor traffic pattern. Finally, and again despite

Helen's artistic talent, the room was poorly lit.

The Mistakes

- Poor furniture placement
- Poor traffic pattern
- Improper use of art
- Ineffective use of accessories
- Ignoring the focal point
- Inadequate lighting

The Remedy

The first thing we did was to flip the sofas so that the higher-backed one is now at the far end of the room to more effectively hide the heating and air-conditioning unit under the window and the lower one is nearest the entrance so that the room appears to be more accessible and open. We also moved the sofas closer together so that it is no longer necessary to raise one's voice or perch at the edge of a seat to carry on a conversation. The two sofas are now anchored on the carpet with the coffee table between them and ac-

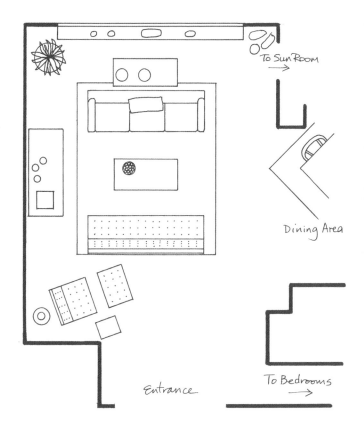

To Sun Room →

Dining Area

Entrance

To Bedrooms →

After

cessible to both. The server on the long left wall, which was originally much closer to the sofa at the far end, is now centered between them for balance.

The dark, midcentury chair that had been standing in the niche near the

dining area and serving no useful purpose was removed. The white Barcelona chair that had been in the far corner near the windows was re-united with its matching ottoman. We moved the desklike table that had been behind the near sofa to behind the far sofa at the opposite end of the room and placed the Barcelona chair and ottoman in the near corner opposite the entrance. We completed this little reading area with a low Asian-style stool, a table, and a lamp, all of which had been near the window. Now Bernard has a cozy and comfortable place to sit and read, and he can use the stool as a resting place for magazines or books. He was thrilled, and I was delighted by his reaction. In addition to creating this privacy nook, however, removing the chairs from the right-hand wall also provided a clear passage from the entrance all the way to the windows.

Next, we tackled the artwork. The five substantial paintings that had been strung in a row along the unbroken wall on the left-hand side of the room were pulled closer together and

All of the art, sculpture, and furniture now work together in a well-balanced arrangement.

◄ After

241

"I never would have thought of that!"

Creating a gallery-like display of the sculpture under the windows: The lesson learned here is that how a collection is displayed can be as important as what is in the collection.

arranged in a single cohesive and balanced grouping above the server, leaving a restful expanse of blank wall on either side. We also moved the three pieces that had been hung, one above the other, on the narrow wall between the windows and the door to the sunroom, which is not visible in the photos, into the master bedroom. Now the eye can settle on the view from the windows and find a place to rest on the adjacent blank wall.

With the paintings repositioned, we were now ready to work with the sculpture, which had been scattered throughout the living room, dining alcove, and entrance hall, diluting their collective impact. We moved a long marble-topped table from the dining room to stand under the window, where it now holds a display of five stone pieces. We then arranged a grouping of several more pieces on the floor in the corner near the sunroom door where the three paintings and the Barcelona chair had been. All the sculpture is now in one area of the room and displayed, gallery-style, to greater and more dramatic effect.

With so much artwork, other accessories needed to be kept to a minimum. We removed everything that had been on the server and replaced those pieces with a single, square wooden pedestal and a single white sculpture that set off the color in the painting above it. On the coffee table, we placed one dark, round pedestal bowl filled with fruit and arranged a few small objects next to it.

Three oriental-type rugs—one between the sofas, one behind the near sofa, and one (not shown in the photos) in the entranceway—also

242

chopped up the space, competed with the art for attention, and contributed to that sense of visual chaos. When we removed those from behind the sofa and in the entrance, the room immediately felt larger and more serene.

The lighting, which was inadequate, could not be totally improved that day, although I was able to provide Bernard with a reading lamp for his corner, and the white torchiere that had been in the back left-hand corner of the room was left to provide general lighting. We raised the jade plants, also in that corner, onto a low Chinese-style bench that had been next to the Barcelona chair, placing them in front of the lamp for a more dramatic effect.

Long-Term Recommendations

To optimize the lighting and show off their art to best advantage, I suggested that the Sokolovs replace the existing track, which was lighting only the near end of the room, with a new one, 8 to 12 feet long, in the center of the ceiling and running parallel to the server so that it could be used to highlight the paintings on the long wall as well as to provide general illumination for the room as a whole.

I also suggested that they buy a pair of black metal or brass pharmacy lamps that could be placed next to the sofas, nearest to the left wall, for task lighting, which would allow them to remove the white torchiere.

Since the Sokolovs had indicated that they were "ready for a new rug," I advised them to purchase a neutral, 8 by 10–foot Tibetan that would compete less with their paintings and sculpture than the heavily patterned oriental.

I also suggested that they consider reupholstering the sofas, one of which was leather and the other fabric, in a mushroom-toned ultrasuede, which would be both neutral and durable and would pick up the color in the new rug.

THE CLIENTS' REACTION

Helen had very definite ideas about the display of their artwork and was initially resistant to my moving *any* of it, but she was willing to listen to my suggestions and once we began to move things around, she was able to understand and appreciate the reasoning. In the end, she was delighted with the results—as was her husband—so much so, in fact, that they asked me to consult on two additional rooms. Once we were done, Bernard remarked that I'd made them "feel young again."

"Our house feels bigger than when you arrived," Helen noted. "Can you believe this? It's amazing!"

21

Views on Retirement

MOVING FROM COAST TO COAST

The Client
and the Complaint

"You walked us through the process for our place in New York," said Dayva Stewart when she called to ask if I'd fly out to consult on the retirement home she and her husband had purchased on a hill high above Laguna Beach, California. "I loved having the written design plan to pull out and refer to whenever I needed it. It worked really well for us. We're really good at following directions."

Dayva is a leggy blonde with a huge, bright smile and blue eyes that

Dayva Stewart and John Shewmaker

light up with enthusiasm when she speaks. Her husband, John Shewmaker, is a tall, slim man with boyish good looks. Both Dayva and John were living and working in New York when they began to look for their dream house in 1992. She's a native Californian and he'd lived there for many years, so they both knew it was where they wanted to retire. But they weren't in any hurry. In fact, it took them

eight years of going to open houses and working with real estate brokers whenever they were on the West Coast. Then, in 2000, they found the perfect place.

Built in 1973, the two-story contemporary is an "upside-down" house, with the main entrance as well as the living room, dining room, kitchen, and master bedroom on the second floor— and with good reason. Although I've

Overlooking the town of Laguna Beach and the Pacific shoreline, this home is all about the view!

Before ▼

decorated many homes in southern California and elsewhere on the West Coast, Dayva and John's 180-degree view overlooking the town of Laguna Beach, the Pacific coastline, and Catalina Island is possibly the most beautiful I've ever seen anywhere. When I first saw it, however, the interior was completely empty except for a couple of director's chairs they had set up in the living room. There was a travertine floor in the entryway, but the rest of the floors were unfinished exposed concrete. My clients wanted to bring some of their things from New York—and since I'd worked with them there I knew what they had—but they really didn't know what would work, how to arrange things, or how to finish their new space.

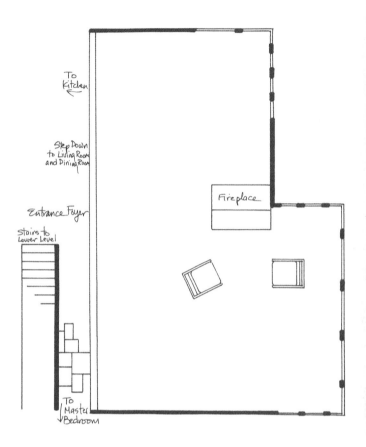

Before

The Diagnosis

Clearly, this home was all about the glass and the view. In fact, there were very few solid walls on the entire top floor. Although I would help them with the whole house, we started with the living/dining room, which was very open, with windows on three walls and glass doors leading out to a veranda. The ceiling was vaulted with exposed beams.

Separating the living and dining areas was a fireplace, which would make

247

Before ▲

While a fireplace is always a welcome element to any room, this one blocked the magnificent view that was a major selling point for this oceanside home.

for very awkward furniture placement if, as is usual, the fireplace was to provide a focal point of the living room. The fireplace definitely belonged on the opposite wall, which also happened to be one of the few solid walls in the room. Dayva and John weren't planning on a major renovation, just some floor and window treatments and advice on furniture placement. But it didn't turn out that way.

Although my clients had never been involved in a major remodeling, they didn't balk, even when, as it turned out, they had to go to the Laguna Beach Design Review Board and agree to a public hearing in order to obtain permission. In fact, while they were at it, they also decided to stucco the outside of the house, which was shingled and looking somewhat worn and dated. In the end, the whole

248

project wasn't completed until three years after they first found the house.

The Remedy

Dayva and John had a bone-colored leather sofa and a matching loveseat from their New York home, which I thought would work well. Assuming that the fireplace would be moved, the sofa could be positioned to face it, with the loveseat at a right angle facing the window wall. They also had two chairs and a matching ottoman that were upholstered in woven, cocoa-colored chenille. The chairs, positioned with their backs to the windows, would complete the U-shaped conversation area, and the ottoman could "float" in the far right corner. Their glass and chrome coffee table would make the move, too, along with two end tables— one in glass and chrome, the other in light wood—and a Tibetan rug. So, in effect, the entire conversation area from their New York living room would re-tire to Laguna Beach with them.

I suggested that they purchase a pair of matching lamps for the end ta-bles and that, sometime in the future, they replace the tables themselves with a matched pair in light wood to match the legs of the chairs.

That left the flooring, general light-ing, and window treatments to con-sider. For both the living and dining rooms I recommended the installation of white oak flooring to run in the same direction as the ceiling beams. For the living room lighting, I thought they should move the existing track to the side of the ceiling beam and use tiny halogen spots to highlight the fireplace wall. They could then install a second track closer to the fireplace for general illumination. They'd have to have some kind of sun protection on the windows, but we all agreed that whatever they got, it shouldn't be a traditional window treatment. My suggestion was a solar film or shade of some kind.

We then moved on to the dining room. The oval cherry dining table and eight Shaker-style chairs would also make the move from New York, as would their lacquered anigre wood server and a second Tibetan rug. I sug-gested that Dayva and John reuphol-

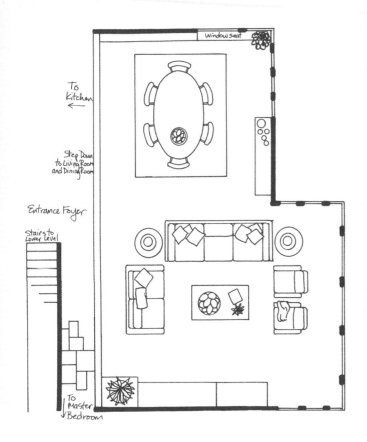

Labels on the plan:
Window seat
To Kitchen
Step Down to Living Room and Dining Room
Entrance Foyer
Stairs to Lower Level
To Master Bedroom

After

ster the chairs in neutral ultrasuede and use only six of the eight they had around the table when they weren't entertaining. They could have tailored slipcovers made for the remaining two in neutral-colored linen or cotton and stand them on either side of the server. Then, if they needed extra seating for dinner guests, they could easily pull the two up to the table. For the back wall, I recommended that they find or have built-in a closed armoire-type piece in which to store their dining room linens, china, and silver. To provide even more storage, I recommended that if they chose the built-in option, they could extend the unit from wall to wall to create a window seat with additional drawers beneath it.

Although Dayva and John had intended to hang a chandelier above the table, I suggested that, because the ceiling wasn't straight, it would be better to install a track parallel to and between two of the beams.

Since there were so few walls and so many windows, as well as the living art provided by the spectacular view, I thought that they ought to be very careful about hanging any art at all. But the one place a painting would work was above the server. So, again, most of the dining room furniture would be traveling cross-country.

▶ We then looked at the bedroom, which is one small step down from the entry hall. We didn't photograph it

▲ After   The fireplace, which now occupies a
much more convenient spot, was a
major piece of the renovation but one
that was certainly worthwhile.

251

that first day because it was, after all, nothing but an empty space. But even empty, I could see that once it was done, it would be spectacular. Like the living room, the bedroom looks out on a panorama of the Pacific coastline. In addition, the entire left side is a wall of closets with mirrored sliding doors that reflect the view.

To match the drama of the "living art," I suggested that Dayva and John find a high, upholstered headboard for their bed. It would not only make a statement but would also provide more comfort for reading in bed (which they both enjoyed) and would help to balance the height of the glass doors and windows on the opposite wall.

They would also need a pair of bedside tables and a pair of lamps as well as another piece that would provide additional closed storage. To the left, on the same wall as the bed, is a small windowed alcove where I recommended that they build a window seat in which to keep extra bedding.

The Ultimate Result

The window treatments that Dayva and John had found and used throughout the entire top floor were solar shades that can be lowered or raised individually by remote control. When they're up, they disappear into a hidden cornice, and when they're down, they blend into the linen white walls so that they're barely noticeable.

In the living room, the fireplace had been moved to the opposite wall, and to the left of it a cabinetmaker had created an entire built-in unit that now holds a large television as well as storage for books and tapes, all hidden behind bifold doors. To the right of the fireplace is a niche in which to store wood and, above that, an open shelf.

The furniture and rug for the conversation area were in place, so we went out to shop for lamps and accessories. The lamps we found for the end tables are an ebony color with bulbous bases and long, thin necks. The green silk shades pick up the touch of green in the dining room rug.

In addition, we found several throw pillows for the sofas: two linen with

▲ After

With the fireplace removed, the view and the traffic pattern are now completely open. The conversation area is furnished for the most part with things brought from the owners' previous home.

raffia edges and two others covered with decorative maplewood disks. Another, which Dayva and John already had, is in a green raw silk that blends perfectly with the lamp shades.

On the coffee table, we arranged a vase of fresh flowers, several art books, and a copper plate with seashells to bring the beach inside. For the shelf to the right of the fireplace, we purchased a large bamboo vase, which we filled with curly branches, and created a vignette with a chrome clock, a porcelain conch shell by a local artist, and a black-framed mirror.

For the dining room, Dayva and John added a built-in closed breakfront with doors above and drawers underneath as well as a window seat with storage below. In white oak with rice-paper insets in the doors, the breakfront has clean, simple lines with a somewhat Asian feeling.

The painting they'd bought to hang above the server is by David Schluss, an Israeli artist who paints with his hands instead of brushes. The only piece of art on the entire top floor, it

The dining area is kept very simple so it does not distract from the "living art" of the panoramic views. A corner window seat (not shown) provides additional seating and storage.

◄ After

255

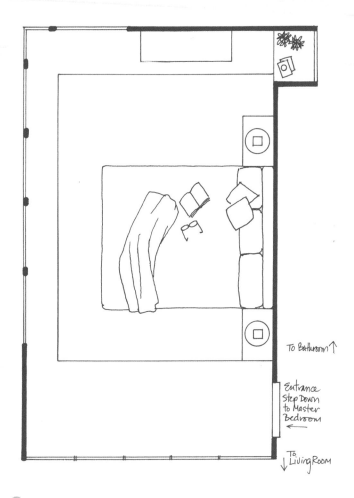

To Bathroom ↑

Entrance
Step Down
to Master
Bedroom
←

To
↓ Living Room

After

Elegant and
understated, the
bedroom is a
serene hideaway.

provides a dramatic splash of bright color in the otherwise neutral rooms.

To accessorize the server, we arranged a grouping of mahogany candlesticks in a variety of interesting shapes, a small greige-colored vase, and a platter that incorporates the colors of the candlesticks as well as the greige of the vase.

We pulled the slipcovered chairs up to either end of the table and stored away two of the plain ones. On the dining table itself I put a white bowl filled with pears, and, on the window seat in the corner, a tall white porcelain vase of flowers.

▶ In the bedroom, both the tufted headboard and smoothly upholstered base of the bed are covered in a toffee-colored chenille, with a chenille throw and decorative pillows in the same color and all-white bedding.

The bedside tables have one large drawer for closed storage above and an open space for books below. The lamps are white porcelain with linen barrel shades, and the armoire Dayva and John bought to put on the one small piece of available wall, is in dark mahogany with tiny steel studs on the front.

Although I'd suggested wall-to-wall carpeting, they'd chosen instead the same wood flooring that was in the other rooms. Under the bed, they had

laid a very beautiful Pakistani rug in a peachy color with a mocha design to pick up the color of the upholstered headboard.

They not only built the window seat I'd recommended but also added a deck that's accessed directly from the bedroom. "People really underestimate how much impact our environments have on us," Dayva commented as we marveled yet again at the view.

THE CLIENTS' REACTION

From the moment they bought it, Dayva and John have been thrilled with their new home. "We made a list of must-haves and would-be-nice-to-haves, and we have virtually everything on both lists," John commented the first time I saw the house. Now they were even more thrilled with the way it has turned out.

"We're living our dream," Dayva told me. "We have to pinch ourselves every day."

"This house is so easy and comfortable," John added. "This is the kind of place you escape to, not from."

And I had to agree with both of them. Their hillside aerie is both sleek and comfortable, and the panoramic "multimillion-dollar view" truly makes you feel as if the whole world were at your feet.

22

Design for Love

MERGING HOUSEHOLDS

The Clients
and the Complaint

"We need to merge. We haven't had friends over. We just didn't know how to do this whole thing. I don't feel this place reflects *me*, and I haven't had a real home since I moved, so it's important to me to have a refuge, especially in the city."

Lorinda is a blonde, blue-eyed California girl from Santa Barbara, and as sweet as you could ever imagine. Gentle, soft-spoken, and willowy, she's studying oriental medicine and plans to open her own practice once she gets her degree. Tavor, originally from Boston, is a management consultant

Lorinda Toscas and Tavor White

who travels all over the world "helping companies grow and reduce their cost structures." Both were divorced when they met at their allergy doctor's office, and Lorinda had moved in with Tavor about a year before they called me.

The transition has been difficult for her because she's used to those open California spaces, and his place was so dark that, as she put it, "I felt like I was living in a cave." But there was more to it than that. Tavor is a collector and, it would seem, has brought home something from every trip he's ever taken. All his things are interesting, but most of them are *big:* voodoo masks, drums, buddhas, carvings, and more. Each piece he buys has a story, and looking at any one of them brings back a flood of memories for him. When I arrived, however, most of them were on the floor, literally lining the perimeter of the living room. "I was trying to work with what he had," Lorinda told me, "but there's just too much stuff here for me."

Making it work had been difficult for both of them, and Tavor was as eager as Lorinda to find a solution. She

had begun to believe that their decorating problems, their inability to mesh in terms of arranging their living space, might be indicative of deeper problems in the relationship. "We have conflicting aesthetics," Lorinda said. "I felt stuck, and I translated that into our relationship because I thought *we* weren't compatible." She felt that, because it was *his* space, she couldn't really assert her opinion as strongly as she would have liked. And he, on the other hand, felt that although he loved her, she was, in a sense, invading his space. "She doesn't appreciate my things," he said, "and each one is part of a cultural experience for me." Clearly, the pieces he'd collected were very important to Tavor, but now Lorinda was very important, too. That was a conflict for him, and he realized that their entire relationship was at stake.

By the time I met them, they'd been going to couples therapy to try to resolve the issue, and, in fact, my being there was a serendipitous result of one of the exercises Tavor had been assigned by their therapist. Lorinda had been told to "fix the place up," and

With an abundance of riches from many years of travel and collecting, this room looks more like a jumble sale than the stylish home that Lorinda and Tavor were desperately seeking.

Tavor had been asked to clean out his office. I'd worked with him several years before, when he was doing a gut renovation on his previous home in New Jersey. Now, he said, "I cleaned out my office, and, two months after the exercise, I came upon this old plan from Use What You Have®. That's really when I thought it was a sign for me to call you back."

The Diagnosis

"I don't have an attachment to these things," Lorinda told me as we got

The sofa, like so many of the handsome pieces in this room, seems to be floating in limbo.

started, "but I'm happy about what we're doing now because it will give Tavor what he needs."

My job was to see that the needs of both were met, and the first thing I told them was that there were certain things they'd need to do if we were to be successful. One of the things Tavor would have to do was to give up—or at least store—some of what he had.

▶ As you enter their space, to the left is the kitchen, with a breakfast bar opening to the living room. Above the

Before ▼

bar there are three pieces of art. Two of the living room walls are exposed brick. The one to the left, perpendicular to the kitchen, has a fireplace, above which hung a gold-leaf mirror. To the left of the fireplace was a grandfather clock and to its right a large armoire that housed their audio/video equipment. There was a large red lacquered pot on top of the armoire, and a chaotic collection of Tavor's artifacts cluttered the floor along the entire length of the wall.

The window wall is opposite the entrance door. To the left of the windows was a small Tibetan cabinet with a Tibetan thangka hanging above it and a large candelabra standing on the floor next to it. To the right of the windows were two more, smaller thangkas, one of them half hidden behind the pedestal table.

Lined up along the other long brick wall was a metal-based table with a framed piece of art resting on top, a plantation-style rattan chaise lounge, and a Noguchi-style lamp behind which stood a large amethyst geode.

The sofa was freestanding in the middle of the room in front of the rat-

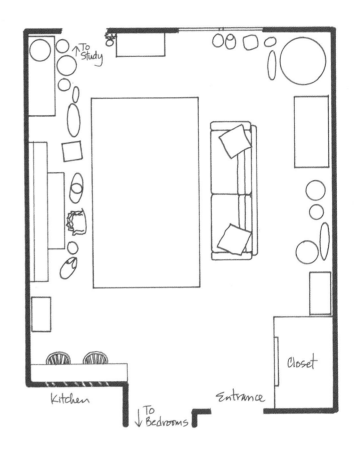

Before

tan lounge and facing the fireplace. On the floor in front of it was a lovely silk rug that is so delicate Lorinda and Tavor told me they walked around the room barefoot in order to protect it. That rug was one of the things I told Tavor he'd have to deal with immediately. I explained that while your pos-

263

sessions are important, they should never be so important that they possess you. For now, they needed to fold up the rug and store it until they had a larger house where they could put it in a room that didn't have so much traffic. For the present, the living room was their main living space, and they needed to find a rug that was more practical and functional.

The sofa, as it turned out, was also a problem. Although they'd chosen it together, when they got it home, Lorinda decided that it had been a mistake but couldn't return it because it had been custom made. The tag was still on the arm when I arrived, and the perception that she'd somehow "messed up" was adding to Lorinda's stress. But the sofa really wasn't bad. It was a neutral color and quite comfortable, and I suggested that when everything else was working better she would probably feel better about it.

The Mistakes

- Improper display of artwork
- Ineffective use of accessories
- Poor furniture placement
- Uncomfortable traffic pattern
- Insufficient lighting
- Lack of focal point

The Remedy

It was obvious to all of us that the most important thing we needed to do was to find a way for Tavor to keep and display the majority of his treasures while also creating a sense of peace and order for Lorinda. The solution to their problem was to get as much as possible *off* the floor, and to do that I recommended that they have a carpenter build them gallery-style shelving along the entire length of the long brick wall on the right. The lower shelf should be high enough from the floor to accommodate larger pieces—at least 32 inches. The shelves needed to be very strong and thick to hold the weight of the heavier pieces; there should be as few visible supports as possible; and the entire unit should be painted with white semigloss to brighten the room.

The brick wall itself was attractive, but it wasn't really being utilized, and making it the backdrop for the gallery display would be not only dramatic but also practical. Lorinda and Tavor would be turning chaos into something organized and aesthetically pleasing while also freeing up floor space for more practical furniture.

The rattan chaise would have to go—at least into storage. The geode, which was hidden behind the Noguchi lamp, could be placed on a black marble pedestal and put to the left of the fireplace. And, finally, they would install a track with small halogen lights to run the entire length of the "gallery" to highlight the collection.

I suggested that they center the sofa directly in front of the gallery shelving with a pair of metal pharmacy lamps on either side for task lighting. To complete the U-shaped conversation area, I recommended that they get an upholstered chair and matching ottoman in a solid-color fabric. For coffee tables, we found two dark-stained cubes with storage inside, in a catalogue. To anchor the space, I suggested

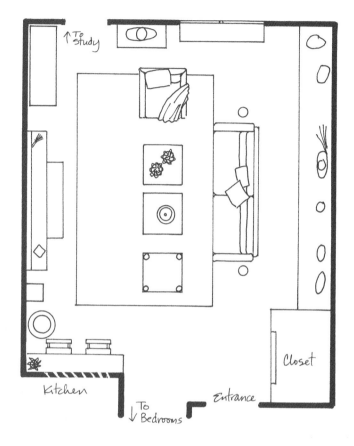

After

a solid neutral-colored flat-weave rug with a dark brown or black cotton border. They could also have a pair of 16-inch throw pillows made in the chair fabric to put on the sofa.

The windows had child guards, which I suggested they remove. I also recommended that they replace the wooden blinds with white pleated shades mounted inside the window frames to lighten up the room. They could then have a window seat built with a bifold door to give them access to the air conditioner on one side and storage on the other. The unit could be painted the same semigloss white as the built-in shelving with a cushion in an accent color to go with the chair and ottoman. The Tibetan cabinet would stay in place, and the walls on either side of the windows left bare.

The armoire would also stay to the right of the fireplace, with nothing on top of it. The grandfather clock and a few other nonessentials could be put into storage. The gold-framed mirror above the fireplace would be replaced with one framed in silver or black. And, to complete the transformation, they'd repaint the trim in white semigloss rather than flat white and repaint the walls in an eggshell-finish white.

When I returned just six weeks later, the gallery shelves had been built and filled with Tavor's most meaningful and precious pieces.

The pharmacy lamps were in place on either side of the sofa with the two-cube coffee table in front. There was now a cherry-red, striped chenille chair to the left of the sofa with its back to the window wall. The matching ottoman they'd ordered wasn't yet ready, so we moved a small white one in from the hall temporarily. A flat-weave, sisal-colored rug with a black border anchors the space. In the future, Lorinda will also purchase a drop-leaf table she can keep behind the sofa and pull out for dinner parties.

On the coffee tables we placed two silver vases with flowers and a covered wooden bowl. On the chair, ottoman, and sofa there were flat Tibetan pillows whose tassels picked up the red of the chair. For the sofa, Lorinda had also found a flat black rectangular Asian pillow in the shop where she purchased the chair, and to go with it,

"I never would have thought of that!"

Building the gallery of shelves: This addition was the key to solving the fundamental problem.

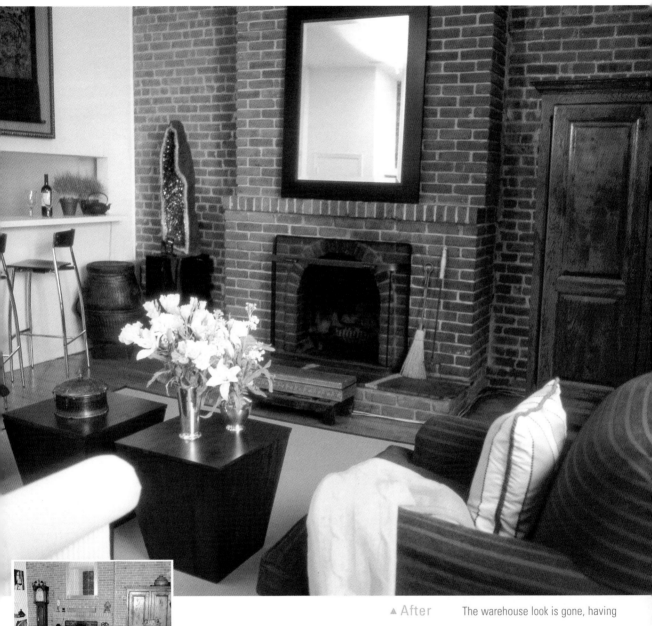

▲ After   The warehouse look is gone, having
been replaced with sophisticated and
cheerful simplicity.

I brought in a square black linen cushion as well as an oatmeal-colored wool throw for the chair.

A dark-stained, covered storage basket is tucked under the breakfast counter along with three ebony and chrome stools. The large thangka has been hung above it. (One of the smaller ones will lean against the wall on one of the display shelves, and the other will be moved to the hallway.)

Above the mantel, a rectangular black-framed mirror balances all the things displayed on the opposite wall. The geode, which now has a tiny up light illuminating its interior, looks beautiful on its pedestal in the corner next to the fireplace. We used the newly built window seat to display a 3-foot-high carved black bird. The Tibetan chest now holds one of Tavor's buddhas, and the red pot has been moved from the top of the armoire to the display shelf. The grandfather clock has gone into storage along with the silk rug, the rattan chaise lounge, and a few other pieces that simply didn't fit in the room.

A few new pieces in a well-balanced arrangement along with a well-designed display case transformed the environment of this room.

After ▶

268

THE CLIENTS' REACTION

This was the perfect solution," Lorinda exclaimed when I returned to see all the work they'd done. "I can't tell you how excited Tavor is now that he has a gallery for his things. It's something he's always wanted. And for me, everything feels so much lighter and more cheerful!

"We're both nature lovers," she went on, "and the new window treatment allows us to see more of the trees and the birds in the backyard. Finally, we feel that we have a real home," she concluded as she looked around.

Tavor, as she said, is overjoyed with the results, and Lorinda now feels that their home reflects her personality also. They both feel that their desires, tastes, and style have been respected. In fact, they are so well merged that they have become engaged to be married.

23
Solid Roots

MAKING A COMMITMENT TO STAY AND REDECORATE

The Client
and the Complaint

"I knew what I wanted, how I wanted the space to feel, but I really needed a pro to pull it together. I'm very busy with my work and my personal life, and I really don't have a lot of time to do this," Vicki said when I arrived at the 3,800-square-foot home she and her husband, Michael, had recently bought in Palm Beach, Florida.

A youthful-looking blonde, Vicki is an attorney and chief legal counsel for a state agency in Palm Beach County. Her husband is a real estate developer whose work requires him to commute

Vicki finally made the decision to stay in Palm Beach and now needed to make her family home feel more permanent.

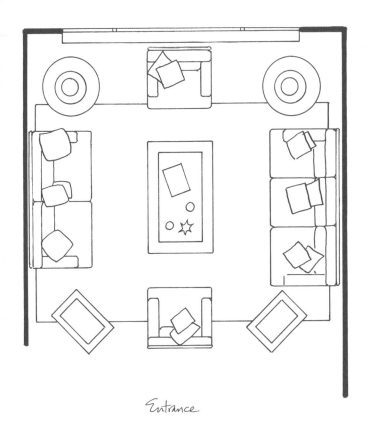

Entrance

moved to a larger home where their daughter, Anastasia, would have more play space and where Vicki and Michael would have more room to entertain. The only problem was that Vicki was so busy with her job and other obligations that she was overwhelmed by the thought of having to get the house together. And because they were making a real commitment to putting down roots, she wanted to do it correctly.

The Diagnosis

The house itself is very beautiful, with a circular driveway, high ceilings, Saturnia marble floors throughout the first floor, and a triple window with an arched top that takes up much of the back wall in the living room. All the rooms on the main floor are accessed from a central entrance foyer that extends all the way back to the family room. The living room is to the right of the entrance foyer, behind a set-back staircase that leads to the second floor. To the left are the study and the dining room.

Before

to Tampa on a regular basis, and because of his commute, Michael and Vicki had been considering a move to Tampa. But there were other considerations, including Vicki's job and their seven-year-old daughter's attachment to her friends in the community, which ultimately determined that they would stay in Palm Beach.

Once the decision was made, they

The living room was very symmetrical and well balanced, with many pairs already in place, and Vicki really did know exactly what she wanted: a clean, pared-down, classic look with light upholstery and accents of aqua, blues, and greens.

The furniture had been arranged almost in a circle around a rectangular, wood-framed, glass-topped coffee table, but none of the seating was within reach of the coffee table. To either side of the window was one of a pair of round, skirted tables covered in a fringed beige moiré fabric, each of which held a pineapple-shaped lamp with a round linen shade. One of a pair of club chairs was centered on the window wall and the other one facing it across the length of the coffee table. There was a loveseat against the left-hand wall with a full-size sofa across from it. All the fabrics were in ivory or cream cotton or silk. The comfortable, boxy club chairs were in a white-on-white fabric with a vine pattern woven through it. The sofa was in a tailored style with comfortable rounded arms, and the loveseat had two overstuffed back cushions and turned arms similar

to those of the sofa. All the seating was of the same height and accessorized with an assortment of throw pillows.

In addition to the skirted tables, a pair of British colonial–style rectangular end tables with shelves below and glass tops were angled on either side of the club chair facing the window.

By far the most beautiful thing in the room, however, was the Egyptian silk rug in shades of green, icy aqua, and taupe that anchored the conversation area. These were the colors Vicki wanted to pull out and use as accent colors, and I thoroughly agreed with her choice.

Before ▼

This elegant and well-appointed room has many of the elements needed to make it work well—lots of pairs and lovely furniture—but just doesn't function well at all.

Although I realized that the balance and symmetry of the room were going to make my job relatively easy, there were problems to be addressed. For one thing, anyone sitting on either the sofa or the loveseat would have to hoist themselves out of his or her seat to reach the coffee table. The end tables that completed the circle of furniture on either side of the club chair were blocking the traffic pattern and creating poor feng shui because the energy couldn't flow into the room. And, finally, the skirted tables, while tasteful and well balanced, were also a bit dated.

I knew that the flimsy, floor-length curtains on the triple window were temporary, but they were obscuring the view that should have been the focal point of the room.

The Mistakes

- Poor furniture placement
- Uncomfortable conversation area
- Obstructed traffic pattern
- Ignoring the focal point
- Ineffective use of accessories
- Lack of artwork

The Remedy

I suggested to Vicki that we needed to open up the traffic pattern and create a more comfortable conversation area that would allow people to sit comfortably facing one another and close enough together so that they could reach the table without lifting off their seats and wouldn't have to raise their voices to be heard.

To create a U shape instead of the closed circle, we moved the sofa so that its back was to the window, moved the loveseat from the left-hand wall to the right side, where the sofa had been, and balanced it with the two club chairs placed in front of the left-hand wall and close enough together so that they were almost touching. We then turned the coffee table so that it was running parallel rather than perpendicular to the windows. And to give the arrangement a more modern look, we moved the skirted tables to the master bedroom and replaced them with the British colonial-style end tables with the pineapple lamps centered on top.

All the seating was now closer together, creating a more intimate and comfortable conversation area, but I suggested that Vicki needed something near the entrance to the room to make it more balanced, interesting, and complete. I thought a desk would be appropriate because it would provide a place for an additional lamp and a pull-up chair as well as somewhere for Vicki to sit, write, pay bills, or whatever.

Serendipitously, Vicki actually had a very nice French wooden desk in the foyer that was really too small for the space. We brought it into the living room and placed it on the right, near the entrance, along with an armless wooden chair that had been in the family room. She also, as it turned out, had a pretty lamp in pale celadon that had been in the bedroom but picked up the blue in the rug and really worked well on the desk. All she would have to do was replace the feminine, "bedroomy" shade with a more tailored, barrel-shaped one.

▶ On to the accessories and artwork. Vicki had two silk pillows that were banana on one side and gold on the

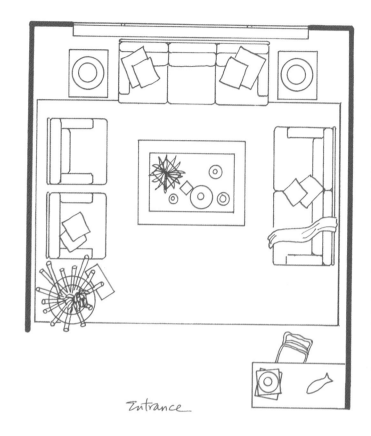

Entrance

After

other, which we placed at either end of the sofa along with its two matching pillows. Scattered about the room she also had three green pillows, two of which we put on the chair farthest from the window. We arranged several pots in various sizes, shapes, and shades of blue on the coffee table. They picked up the colors in the rug, acknowledged the lamp on the desk,

275

and looked not only very beautiful but also quite important once they were gathered in one place.

Vicki told me she had an oil painting of a garden scene in a gold-leaf frame that she'd been thinking of hanging in the living room. When we looked at it, however, I thought it would work better in the bedroom. Instead, I chose a tranquil beach scene in neutrals, celadon, and greens in a silver-leaf frame, which she'd been waiting to hang because she wasn't sure where to place it, and hung it on the left-hand wall behind one of the club chairs. She also had two unframed prints—one a nude and the other a still life—that were the same size and by the same artist, which she would have framed in silver leaf and hang one above the other on the right-hand wall, parallel to the desk chair, for balance.

Long-Term Recommendations

Because the living room windows are so dramatic and the large palm trees centered outside are so attractive, I suggested that Vicki remove the temporary curtains and open up the view. Ultimately, she could have solid raw-silk panels made in green or icy blue that could be pulled in if she wanted to block some of the light.

I also recommended that she have the sofa and loveseat reupholstered in silk or cotton and slipcover the chairs in solid linen for a fresher look. In addition, I thought she should replace the wooden desk chair with one that had a seat and back upholstered in ice-blue raw silk. If she did that, she could also have a couple of throw pillows made in the same fabric to use in the conversation area.

"I never would have thought of that!"

Putting the club chairs side by side: "I always thought you had to separate the chairs," confessed Vicki. "And also, I never would have shaped the seating that way with the coffee table running parallel to the windows and the end tables on the sides. And I never would have put the desk where it is or the painting where it is!"

▲ After   It is remarkable what a difference a
few simple changes can make imme-
diately. Removal of the drapery
revealed a painterly scene that gave
the room its dramatic focal point.

Just a week after the initial consultation, the room has already come a long way with the addition of a few deep-toned accents.

In addition to framing and hanging the prints and replacing the shade on the desk lamp, the room still needed a few accessories to pull it together, and because Vicki was so busy, she asked me to do the shopping for her.

When I returned a week later, it was too soon for the furniture to have been recovered, but we talked some more about the window treatments, and I suggested that, in addition to the raw-silk panels, she also order triple-width sheer ecru curtains going from end to end across the high point of the arch to provide sun protection and prevent the rug from fading. But even without those changes, once the new accessories I brought with me were in place, the room looked very much as it ultimately would.

For the near end of the left-hand wall, close to the painting, I found a large hammered copper urn, which I filled with large bamboo poles and bunches of "bananas." The copper picks up one of the colors in the rug, and the bananas are an amusing conversation piece. Next to it, I placed a small black and bamboo Asian-style bench to complete the vignette.

After ▶

278

For the coffee table I found a crackle-glazed porcelain pot, which I filled with orchids, and a mahogany Asian-style tray.

I also brought in a pale sage cut-velvet throw with mocha tassels—all colors that are in the rug—to place on the loveseat. Vicki already had the two green velvet pillows we put on the loveseat and the two in sea foam green for the chairs. For the sofa I found two large pillows in ice-blue linen and two smaller mocha ones in raw silk, which I arranged one in back of the other at either end. Vicki was particularly thrilled with the blue pillows, which, she said, were exactly the color she'd been dreaming of, and seeing her reaction reminded me how big a difference small touches can make in a room.

To complete the new look, I arranged three family photos in silver frames on the end table to the left of the sofa and placed a dark mahogany Asian fish I had found as an accessory on the desk.

THE CLIENT'S REACTION

At the end of my initial visit, Vicki was already delighted and couldn't wait for her husband to get home and see what we'd done. "Oh, my gosh," she exclaimed. "It looks so beautiful! I never would have thought to arrange the furniture this way, but it looks just great." When she remarked upon how balanced it felt, I let her know that by having so many pairs in the room to begin with she'd already done a lot of the work. Pairs will go with you wherever you move and will always work beautifully in any room.

After the second visit, she remarked: "When we decided to buy this house, we knew it was right for us, but we were concerned about whether the things we had would look good here. Now neither one of us can believe what good use we're making of the furniture we already had."

24

Breathing Room

CREATING A HOME SANCTUARY

The Client
and the Complaint

"I can't tell you how happy I am to meet you and finally be able to do this. Obviously it has been a long road just to get to this point."

Lorene Wozniak's situation is, beyond doubt, unique among my clients, and she herself is one of the most inspirational people I've ever met. In 1980 Lorene was about thirty years old, an aggressive Wall Street stockbroker living a fast-paced New York life. One rainy night, as she was crossing the street with a friend who was to be married the following day, a car hit

Lorene Wozniak

both women, killing her friend and dragging Lorene for two blocks before leaving her in a coma with a serious spinal injury. At first, her doctors didn't expect her to survive, and she spent a year in the hospital followed by another year and a half in rehab. At that time, she told God that if she were able to walk again, she would "give back" for what she'd been given, and, when she actually did recover and was released, she enrolled in nursing school and became a clinical nurse specialist.

Her new career took her to many different companies and many different countries, and on the morning of September 11, 2001, it took her to an interview on the fifty-third floor of the World Trade Center. After the attack, she was dragged from the building very badly injured, and before she lost consciousness, she remembers feeling frustrated because, despite all her training, she'd been unable to help any of the people upstairs who lay injured and dying around her. She herself was unconscious for five days and in the hospital for six months.

Before that second tragedy Lorene had called Use What You Have® to book a consultation for mid-September. On September 14 her sister, who had taken the responsibility of checking Lorene's calendar, phoned me to cancel her appointment. I called for months, trying to find out how Lorene was, but I heard nothing more until early 2003, when, for the first time, Lorene's daughter answered the phone. She said that her mother was, fortunately, recovering but was still in rehab. So I asked her to let me know when her mother was well enough for me to come redecorate and cheer her up.

When I arrived at her home several months later she was still walking with a cane but was determined to, as she put it, "pull myself together and get back to normal as much as possible." Now fifty-two years old and twice divorced, with one daughter and two granddaughters, she has enormous energy, a beautiful dancer's carriage in spite of her limp, and a palpable sensitivity to her surroundings.

Hardly a complainer by anyone's standards, Lorene had originally called me because she wanted to bring as much serenity as possible to her sur-roundings, and now, after her second near-death experience, finding that kind of peace was even more impor-tant to her than ever. We were going to work on her living room and dining area, and I took a class of decorator trainees with me because I assumed that she wouldn't be able to help me move furniture if necessary.

The Diagnosis

Despite the fact that she'd made sev-eral of the most common decorating mistakes, Lorene's home already had a lovely warm feeling, almost like a co-coon, with an overstuffed sofa and chairs in the living room and a definite Asian influence.

At the far end of the living room there was a large window with a valance and curtains that should have been—but was not—the focal point of the room. In front of the window Lorene had placed a round, skirted table that held a lamp and a few acces-sories. To the right of the skirted table were a slipper chair and matching ot-

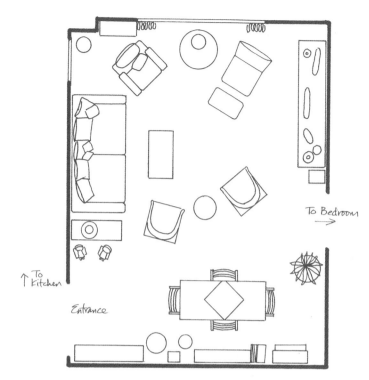

Before

toman. A dark wooden plaque with angels painted on it by a friend hung above the slipper chair. On the wall beside the chair perpendicular to the window was a light maple wall unit that held a variety of collectibles with several accessories on top.

To the left of the large window was a smaller window, and, in the corner between the two, she'd put a small

283

Before ▲

The living room is like a warm cocoon, but with too many things, a lack of cohesion, and poor furniture placement, it feels more chaotic than inviting.

bookcase with a black metal torchiere lamp behind it. A small painting hung on the narrow wall between the two windows. In front of the bookcase was a saddle-colored leather recliner that a former boyfriend had lounged in to watch television but Lorene had always hated.

The sofa, covered in a fabric that coordinated with the slipper chair, was on the left-hand wall next to the smaller window and to its left a glass-topped Parsons table that served as an end table. On top of the table were a lamp and a group of framed photographs; underneath it, her granddaughters' Raggedy Ann dolls and doll furniture. Above the table hung a print that appeared to be floating by itself on the otherwise empty wall. The small rectangular coffee table in front of the sofa had a wrought-iron base and a marble top. Completing the con-

versation area, at right angles to the sofa, were two wooden Chinese chairs with seat cushions and between them a very small Chinese garden bench serving as a table. The chairs were, however, placed so far apart that the small table was almost inaccessible to

The room is off-balance with poor traffic patterns, but with some modest adjustments and careful editing, it will all come together.

Before ▼

285

either one, and conversation with anyone seated on the sofa would be very awkward. They also blocked the traffic pattern for anyone wanting to enter the room.

In addition to the uncomfortable conversation area and poor traffic pattern, there were too many different styles fighting one another in a single space. There were an overstuffed, slip-covered sofa and slipper chair, two spare and Asian wooden chairs and a garden bench, as well as modern tables, traditional and modern lamps, and a leather recliner. Individually, most of these things were attractive, and it was obvious that Lorene had a discerning eye, but the room lacked cohesion.

Some clever solutions are in order to make the dining area more attractive and functional.

Before ▼

286

The dining area—actually an extension of the living room—is opposite the large window, on the wall parallel to and to the right of the entrance. Against the wall there was a tall, black-painted bookcase with a folded-up screen leaning against its left side. In the corner next to that, Lorene had tucked her computer station because, having read my second book, she knew that it didn't belong in her bedroom but didn't know what else to do with it. She was, however, unhappy that she had to see it even when it wasn't in use. Against the wall to the right of the bookcase was another torchiere lamp, a basket holding more toys, and a bag of golf clubs. Lorene told me that she loved Scotland, had played golf there, and kept the golf clubs where she could see them so that they'd inspire her to complete her recovery and be able to play again.

On the short wall at right angles to the computer she had hung a vertical Asian watercolor depicting a small boy and a tree. On the floor near the painting was a schefflera plant for good luck and an urn holding sticks of bamboo. Lorene told me that she sat on a cushion in front of the painting to meditate.

The small, black dining table and four black chairs were in front of and parallel to the bookcase.

The Mistakes:
- Poor furniture placement
- Uncomfortable conversation area
- Poor traffic pattern
- Lack of cohesion
- Improper use of artwork
- Ineffective display of accessories

The Remedy

The first thing we did was to go through the living room furnishings piece by piece to determine what to use and what to discard. Lorene was happy to be rid of the recliner and would also replace the small metal Parsons table next to the sofa.

The parquet floor had been bare, but she did have a lovely silk area rug

287

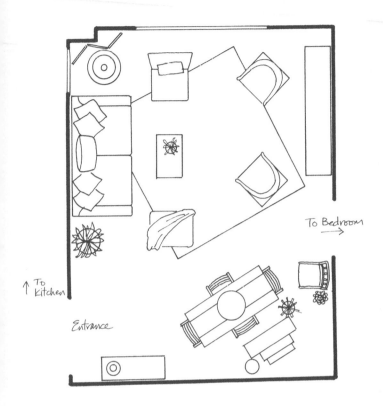

To Bedroom
→

↑ To Kitchen

Entrance

After

into the conversation area, we created a more open and welcoming feeling than when the backs of the two wood chairs had been facing you as you entered the room. We then placed the Chinese chairs at an angle in front of the wall unit so that they could be pulled into the conversation area as necessary. This arrangement also left the traffic pattern much more open than it had been originally.

The unused screen that had been leaning against the bookcase was set up in the corner between the two windows, where it filled the empty space and also balanced the dark wood of the chairs on the other side of the room. We moved the round skirted table to the corner, in front of the screen and next to the sofa, with the traditional table lamp and a group of interesting accessories, including a Chinese box, a piece of Native Indian sculpture, and a small plant on top. We moved the schefflera plant and a Thai sculpture that had been in the bedroom to the opposite side of the sofa for balance and removed the valance from the window.

in celadon, cappuccino, salmon, cream, and taupe that had been cleaned and not yet relaid. We unrolled and positioned it at an angle, sweeping from left to right in front of the sofa, and we moved the slipper chair and ottoman to form a U at either side. With the ottoman at the end closest to the entrance and the angled rug drawing you

▲ After

Everything that Lorene needed to make her home a serene and comfortable haven was already there; she just couldn't see it for the clutter.

289

The unusual arrangement of the Chinese prints balances the small window to the right of the sofa. (A new end table, lamp, and simple accessories will eventually be placed to the left of the sofa to balance those on the right.)

After ▸

To create a cleaner, more cohesive, and relaxing look, we removed everything except the audio speakers from the top of the wall unit and rearranged the accessories on the shelves in groups of like objects.

We moved the print that had been hanging above the Parsons table to the hallway leading to the bedroom along with several angel paintings that had been lost in the living room. Instead, Lorene took out four Asian prints with matching mats and gold-leaf frames that had been stored away, and we hung them vertically, almost floor to ceiling, on the left side of the sofa nearest the entrance, leaving space for the end table she would buy to replace the Parsons table. It was an unconventional use of art, but because of the small window at the far end of the room, she couldn't hang art over the sofa. Leaving that space blank created a place for the eye to rest, and the prints created a strong vertical line to balance the window. Lorene was delighted with the effect.

▸ Moving on to the dining area, I had a really crazy idea. Keeping the

290

"I never would have thought of that!"

Angling the bookcase in the dining room to create an unobtrusive workspace for the computer station with a photo gallery on the exposed side.

After ▾

computer out of sight was very important to Lorene, and it suddenly struck me that if we angled the bookcase away from the wall in the corner farthest from the entrance, we could create a small privacy niche for the computer where no one could see it. We moved the workstation up against the back of the bookcase and set the golf clubs to the right of it, where they would conceal the computer and still be visible to Lorene for inspiration. To the left we placed the urn holding the bamboo. Behind the computer station, we put a folding chair (later to be replaced by a proper desk chair) and, behind that, one of the torchiere lamps. Lorene could still see the entire living room, including the window, when she was working in her little hideaway so it wouldn't feel claustrophobic, and she was absolutely overjoyed by the unique solution to her problem. There comes a time in almost every consultation when the client says, "I never would have thought of that," and this was Lorene's moment.

Next, we removed everything from the bookcase and created a photo gallery, grouped according to the finish of the frames. Lorene would have those that didn't match reframed to complete the effect.

We changed the position of the dining table to run parallel with the angled bookcase, and when I lamented out loud that she didn't have a runner to finish the look, Lorene exclaimed that she did, in fact, have one but had never known what to do with it. We draped it the length of the table and added a flat woven basket, taken from the top of the wall unit, which she would fill with seasonal displays.

Finally, we took a potted plant, which had also been on top of the wall unit, and set it on the garden stool, which I placed under the Chinese painting. Next to that, I angled a pretty old chair Lorene had had in the bedroom, which could be used either as a desk chair or as an additional pull-up chair for company.

Long-Term Recommendations

To complete the window treatment, I suggested that Lorene remove the curtains and the sheers, which fell midway between the sill and the floor, and replace them with off-white or ecru sheers that hung all the way to the floor.

To create better balance and a more cohesive look for the conversation area, she would buy a pair of matching end tables in a wood finish to tie in with the light maple wall unit as well as a pair of matching ginger jar table lamps in hammered steel, celadon, or any solid color that tied in with the rug. If the tables included closed storage underneath for her granddaughters' toys, she could then do away with the basket and the dolls under the table.

For the top of the coffee table I also recommended that she purchase a larger, oval piece of marble in chocolate-colored dark emperador marble or beige travertine to tie in with the other neutrals in the room.

far left: The freestanding bookshelf has been angled out from the corner to create an ideal hidden niche for the computer table—a clever solution in the Use What You Have® tradition.

293

If she were to replace her dining room set, I suggested that she buy a pedestal table, which would take up less room, with leaves that could be added if necessary, and four armless chairs, all in either black, to tie in with the bookcase, or a light wood, to tie in with the living room wall unit.

Finally, I suggested that she use attractive brass tacks to hang a piece of black cloth from the second-to-bottom shelf of the bookcase so that it covered the bottom shelf, which could then be used as closed storage for dining room serving pieces.

But something about seeing the entrance door from the living room and dining area was still bothering Lorene, so I suggested that she purchase a solid-color curtain to hang across the small ceiling beam by the front door and tie it back on the wall where the four vertical prints were hung. If she wanted to, she could then drop the curtain so that it hid the entrance entirely.

THE CLIENT'S REACTION

You have no idea what this means to me." Lorene beamed when we were done. "I just can't stop smiling. Everything looks so elegant, and all the things that were bothering me about the room are gone. I really think what we did today is going to be the start of a wonderful transition into the next stage of my life. I can't thank you enough."

25

Bedtime Story

SEEKING A SERENE ENVIRONMENT

Alice Sachs Zimet, an inveterate
collector of vintage photos, with
some of her prized pieces.

The Client
and the Complaint

"I love my art, I love my furniture, I
have great things, but I'm totally exasperated. There's so much here, on the
walls, on the floor—everywhere—that
I don't know where to put it! Plus, I
now have a home office with an assistant, and I need space for that, too.
The bottom line is I just can't live like
this anymore."

Alice Zimet is a petite and vivacious
woman in her mid-fifties who smiles a
lot and isn't ever at a loss for words.
She has many friends and enjoys en-

Alice's bedroom was overcrowded with a disparate collection of furniture, art, and accessories.

tertaining at home. She is also the great-granddaughter of the founder of one of our country's preeminent banking institutions and has inherited many fine pieces of nineteenth- and early-twentieth-century furniture as well as many beautiful and valuable accessories, some dating back to the sixteenth century.

In addition to these inherited pieces, Alice's apartment is filled with her own vast, museum-quality collection of nineteenth- and twentieth-century photographs, most of which are black

Before ▼

and white, as well as a large number of family photographs from the same period, which are very dear to her. Considered an expert, she sits on the committee to select the photographic art for Harvard University's permanent collection.

Three years ago, she started her own business consulting with non-profit organizations on how to improve their fund-raising through various corporations. Although she spends a great deal of time lecturing at museums, she's been spending much more time working in a home office she carved out of the dining room in her apartment. She also has a room on another floor of her building that was originally intended to house the tenants' domestic help that she hopes to use as an auxiliary office.

When she called Use What You Have®, Alice said that she was beginning to feel overwhelmed by her artwork, that she was uncomfortable in her apartment because she needed more "visual tranquillity" but that, as a collector, she found it difficult to part with any of what she had.

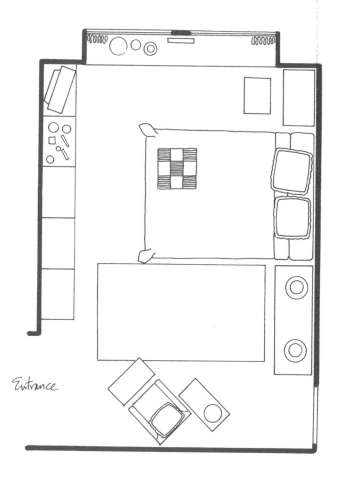

Before

I worked with her on virtually every room of the house, including the kitchen, but the one transformation that gave her immediate pleasure because we could effect a change so quickly was in the bedroom.

297

Another view of Alice's bedroom before the re-configuration.

Before ▲

The Diagnosis

A queen-size bed with no headboard was flanked on one side by a beautiful marble-topped chest that was, nevertheless, very high and very cumbersome, and on the other by a small chest that was a better scale for a bedside table. A wooden curio shelf that held a collection of tiny china cups and saucers she'd been given by her family over the years hung above the small chest. At either end of the bigger chest stood a pair of lamps that Alice's mother had made. They had matching Lucite bases with conch shells mounted on them, but one of them was about ten inches shorter than the other.

The floral curtains were too busy and distracting from the art and other accessories in the room, but she'd already purchased sheeting in a shade of green somewhere between sage and celery that complemented the walls and that she intended to have made into curtains. The color would also work well with the celadon gathered valance that was already in place.

Against the wall across from the bed was a long, built-in piece of furniture that Alice used as a bureau. It had a nice wood top, and the front was painted white. Above this hung a very feminine and fragile oval mirror painted off-white with little flowers and green leaves all around it that she'd inherited from her great-grandfather. Two large colored photographs framed in a light wood finish hung asymmetrically, flanking the mirror. The top of the bureau itself was cluttered with a lot of bits and pieces arranged in no particular order. There were many small boxes of various shapes and materials that actually constituted a collection but weren't

displayed as such, and, at one end, a television.

The fourth wall, opposite the windows, was filled with art hung rather haphazardly above a small, heavily patterned club chair that clashed with the other, softer colors in the room. Next to the chair stood an ornate lamp with a bulbous shade on top of a small trunk.

Finally, on the ceiling, centered over the bed was a modern fixture holding three small lights suspended from what looked like chrome "stalactites" that was so jarringly out of place that it immediately drew your attention.

The Mistakes

- Poor furniture placement
- Inadequate lighting
- Improper use of artwork
- Ineffective use of accessories
- Lack of balance
- Lack of cohesion

The Remedy

A beautiful dresser, now nicely appointed, becomes a focal point for the reconfigured bedroom.

The first thing we did was to move the marble-topped chest from the side of the bed to the wall where the chair had stood. Over it we placed the oval mirror, which I suggested Alice have painted dark brown to complement the wood of the chest below it, leaving just the white flowers and the green leaves intact. On cither side of the mirror we hung a black-and-white photo in a dark wood frame. On top of the chest we placed two small Italian lamps in floral porcelain that were different sizes but complemented one an-

After ▲

other and provided good light. Putting the lamps together was a bit unorthodox, but it worked. Then we found an oval mirror about a foot long, which we placed on top of the chest to serve as a tray. On the tray we arranged a small collection of antique perfume bottles, a couple of pieces of amethyst and lavender glass, and a few small porcelain pots that held lipsticks and jewelry Alice wore frequently.

Next, we brought in a small neoclassical, drop-leaf table from the dining room and put it next to the bed where the larger chest had been. It was similar in height to the small chest on the other side of the bed, and the two woods worked well together. With one of the drop leaves flipped up, it provided a large enough surface to serve as a bedside table.

We placed the Lucite lamps on either side of the bed and put a couple of art books under the shorter one so that they were now of equal height. Their three-way bulbs provided plenty of light, and I suggested that Alice remove the inappropriate ceiling fixture and either cap it or, if she really didn't think the room was light enough, re-

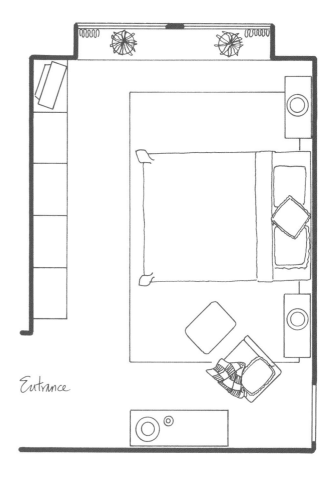

Entrance

After

place it with three small flush-mounted halogen spotlights.

We moved the curio shelf to the dining room, where the food-related porcelains would be displayed more appropriately. And Alice replaced the pile of sweaters that had been on top of the small chest with a collection of stuffed animals from childhood that was aesthetically more pleasing than the sweaters.

A couple of patterned throw pillows brought in from the living room worked well with her solid duvet cover. And I showed her how to make the bed more attractive by folding the sheet over the duvet at the head.

We draped some of the green sheeting she had already bought to make curtains over the patterned club chair and moved the chair along with an ottoman we found in another room next to the drop-leaf table on an angle with both the bed and the television that was on top of the bureau.

That left the wall across from the bed with the built-in bureau. First we cleared the clutter from the top, creating little vignettes by using some of Alice's very best boxes and arranging them in groups that were variations on a theme but leaving as much open space as possible. Then we removed the TV stand from under the television so that it didn't look so high.

The finishing touch was to replace the small area rug to one side of the bed with a larger, chain-stitch floral rug in cream, greens, and raspberry that Alice hadn't been using and that fit perfectly under the bed with a generous "overhang" on either side.

Long-Term Recommendations

Alice wanted more plants on the windowsill to create a garden effect, but the enclosure for the air-conditioning and heating units was too small to accommodate more than one or two. I suggested that she build a new, larger enclosure that would be painted the same color as the walls and covered with a glass top to protect it from the plants she'd be keeping there.

With the mirror above the bureau

"I never would have thought of that!"

Building the floating storage cabinet above the bureau and using the large needlepoint rug under the bed instead of buying two small rugs for either side.

▲ After

In little more than an hour this room
has come a long way to being the
comfortable refuge that Alice was
looking to create.

gone, that wall was empty. Since Alice needed lots of additional storage, I explained to her that "air" always equals potential storage space. My suggestion was that she have a floating cabinet built above the bureau to run the entire length of the lower piece. It would start about two feet above the bureau surface and go all the way up to the picture molding, providing abundant storage space. And, painted in a semigloss finish to match the bottom built-in bureau, it would fade into the background and create some much-needed tranquillity. I also suggested that she cover the empty wall space between the top of the bureau and the bottom of the new floating cabinet with plain mirrored glass, which would not only make the room look more spacious but would also reflect the box collection on top of the bureau.

Finally, to "finish" the bed, I suggested that Alice buy two European square pillows and two tailored solid shams to stand against the wall in place of a headboard. And, to make the bed a principal focal point, she may wish to have a couple of her large photographs reframed in dark wood to hang side by side above the bed.

THE CLIENT'S REACTION

Alice was delighted to see that we'd been able to create tranquillity from chaos while making use of virtually all her furnishings, art, and accessories. She was thrilled to be using all these pieces in such different, more functional ways and to see how well they worked together. "Whoever would have thought that this room could look the way it did at four-thirty and like this at six o'clock? Even though I witnessed it, I can't believe my eyes," she said. She was also very surprised that I had managed to find the storage space she so desperately needed but hadn't been able to envision for herself. The collector in her would now be at peace with the aesthetician.

In 1981, Lauri Ward founded Use What You Have®, Inc., to provide people who didn't think they could afford to hire an interior designer with fast, simple, affordable decorating makeovers. Use What You Have® revolutionized the interior design business, and today Ward is recognized as the pioneer of one-day redecorating and redesign. She is the cofounder, with her husband, Joe Ward, of the Interior Refiners Network®, which has members in more than one hundred cities throughout the United States, Canada, Mexico, Europe, and Australia, and she directs the decorator training program for the IRN® organization.

Ward has appeared frequently on such programs as *The Oprah Winfrey Show, Today,* ABC-TV news, and *CBS Evening News,* as well as shows on HGTV, CNBC, the Discovery Channel, and Fox network. She has been featured in the *New York Times, House Beautiful, Metropolitan Home, Elle, Ladies' Home Journal, Inspired House,* and many other newspapers and magazines. Ward is a contributing home design expert for ivillage.com and a popular speaker and lecturer throughout the United States, committed to educating the public and professionals about interior decorating and thereby helping to make the world a more beautiful, tranquil place, one room at a time.

Visit the Use What You Have® website at *www.redecorate.com* and the Interior Refiners Network website at www.interiorRefiners.com.

Home Therapy?
The "doctor" is in. . . .

**Practical, inspiring advice to transform
your home from Lauri Ward**

Use What You Have® Decorating

*Trade Secrets from Use What
You Have® Decorating*

**Now available in paperback
wherever books are sold.**

For more information about Use What You Have® consultations,
Decorator Training Programs, seminars, and the Interior Refiners
Network®, or to share your before-and-after stories and photos,
please visit www.redecorate.com, www.InteriorRefiners.com, or call
800-WE-USE-IT.